In a world where the message of Jesus can be dumbed down into being just another feel-good consumer product, Clive Calver calls us back to the fabulous upheaval and daily revolution that is the cross-centered life. Timely and incisive, yet warm and kind, Calver charms rather than chides. But make no mistake: this is nothing less than life-changing.

Jeff Lucas
Author, Speaker, Broadcaster

In his new book, *Dying to Live*, Clive Calver brings the reality of his life experience in dynamic fashion backed up with powerful, biblical exposition and application. He invites you to a closer relationship, seeking God for yourself, and God alone. You will be challenged with the centrality of the message of the cross and bringing all of life in line with the gospel. The fullness of Christ's work as Savior and Lord leads you to be a risk-taker and provides a practical challenge for life transformation as you die to live so that you will never die.

David M. Midwood
President
Vision New England

I have known Clive since my student days, and we've traveled countless miles and stood on numerous platforms together. I've watched the path he has taken and shared in many of his joys and sorrows, as he has in mine. I can assure you that this is not just another book, but the record of a quest for authentic Christianity.

With wisdom and compassion, Clive strips off the layers of "lacquer" that have obscured the rough wood of the cross and rendered it safe from the splinters that might pierce our comfort-loving flesh or disturb our religious consumerism. If you too are searching for the real thing, read on.

Graham Kendrick
International worship leader, speaker, and performer
One of the founders and the songwriter behind the global phenomenon
March for Jesus

The examples of everyday men and women throughout this book help the reader to realize that a follower of Christ who has died to himself will be a life-giver not only to the spiritually needy community in North America but also to those whose lives and hopes have been devastated by imposed poverty or by natural or man-made disasters such as genocides and ethnic cleansing in many countries where Dr. Calver has followed Christ. *Dying to Live* is an inspiration showing how a surrendered and Christ-centered life results in changed lives for eternity.

Celestin Musekura
President and CEO
African Leadership And Reconciliation Ministries, Inc.

DYING TO LIVE

DYING TO LIVE

THE PARADOX OF THE CRUCIFIED LIFE

CLIVE CALVER

Authentic

COLORADO SPRINGS • MILTON KEYNES • HYDERABAD

Authentic Publishing
We welcome your questions and comments.

USA   1820 Jet Stream Drive, Colorado Springs, CO 80921
         www.authenticbooks.com
UK   9 Holdom Avenue, Bletchley, Milton Keynes, Bucks, MK1 1QR
         www.authenticmedia.co.uk
India   Logos Bhavan, Medchal Road, Jeedimetla Village, Secunderabad
         500 055, A.P.

Dying to Live
ISBN: 978-1-934068-80-9

Copyright © 2009 by Clive Calver

11 10 09 / 6 5 4 3 2 1

Published in 2009 by Authentic
A catalog record for this book is available through the Library of Congress.

Cover and interior design: projectluz.com
Editorial team: Andy Sloan, Michaela Dodd, Dana Bromley

Printed in the United States of America

Dedication

There are four small groups of people with whom I pray:

The "Elms"—leaders and learners in our community

The "Bulldogs"—those of unique determination to keep going with me

The "Elders"—those who share authority and accountability within the local church, even at 6 AM!

The "Blokes"—those shaping each other, together, for twenty-seven years

To each I am deeply grateful and dedicate this book as a statement of a shared desire: to teach each other what it means to live a more crucified life.

Table of Contents

Foreword

In the first years of our ministry, Becky and I lived in a parsonage (a house supplied by the church). It was very small and very leaky. But we were so thrilled to be married and to have someplace to live that we didn't notice those little imperfections. I earned only a few thousand dollars a year, so we thought this house was a palace! It even had a garbage disposal. How rich we felt having a machine in our sink that would grind up all the garbage and make it go away!

One day the garbage disposal stopped working. The garbage started decaying, and life was getting smelly. We did not think we could afford a licensed plumber to fix the problem. So I tried everything I knew to "unstick" the disposal. But I am not mechanically inclined (that is an understatement), and nothing was working. Life became quite unpleasant with the odor of what was in the disposal and with the work of "taking out the garbage" of daily. Finally, we didn't care what it cost; we had to call for trained help.

The plumber came to our house, went straight to the kitchen, looked under the sink at the disposal motor, hit a red button that read "reset," flipped on the switch above the sink, and the powerful garbage disposal worked as good as new! He then looked at me and said, "That will be fifty dollars."

It was an expensive lesson that has never left me. Since that time, the first thing I look for in anything that is not working is a "reset" button.

This book is one giant reset button for the most important area of your life.

Most of us first trust Christ because we finally realize that we need God to do for us, and in us, and through us what we cannot do on our own. And so there is a great deal of relief, even exhilaration, when we trust that Christ has paid for our sins and we invite the Christ who made the universe to fill us with his life!

But then something happens that indicates our live is again not working so well. So we take over and try to fix what we know nothing about, and life gets filled with the very garbage God had taken away.

Clive Calver is about to remind us of something we have the power to do: hit the "reset" button. Re-depend on Christ. Re-focus on him and his life in us. His power will be re-engaged. And it's free (as well as freeing)!

Dr. Calver is just the right one to take us on this journey back to the original and powerful Way, Truth, and Life. He has led great ministry organizations, such as World Relief, which cares for the most destitute. He has written many books of spiritual insight. He is pastoring a church in which he shepherds people's souls. These qualifications might fit our need: we are desperate people looking for spiritual insight that will lead us to God's care.

Remember as you read this book that it speaks to a very personal journey. Clive does not write as an academic, but as one who is as needy as we are. Ultimately, the Christian life is not about what is or is not working; it is rather about who we really are in Christ, and who he is in us. The Christian life is not mechanical; it is personal. And the life God has for us is not about being good, it is about being loved.

I will be reading this book with you. It seems that I need the "reset" button quite often too. May the person and power of God fill our lives and clear away the garbage.

Joel C. Hunter, D. Min.
Senior Pastor, Northland—A Church Distributed

Thank You

Eucharizomai is the Greek word for "thankful."

Today is Thanksgiving Day and therefore very appropriate. No book can be a "solo" effort, and this one certainly is not.

Charizomai means "to give" and *eu* means "good"; so together they mean "to give good," "to show kindness," or "a good gift." On this Thanksgiving I want to acknowledge those who contributed their love and kindness in the hope that this book would result as "a good gift."

So I express gratitude to Alison and the Authentic team in the U.K. who began the process and to Volney, Dana, and the U.S. Authentic Publishing Group who kept going with me through the good times and the not so good. Volney, your encouragement and commitment were stellar; I am so grateful.

Serving a local church has given to Ruth and me so many reasons for joy. One of the greatest is sharing life with so many others. This was certainly true of the book. Matt Baumgartner and Jamie Marshall researched the "Parabolani." Donna Budd, Bev Carr, Marguerite Enslin, Dr. Jey Jeyapalan, Laura Kennedy, and Rich Rardin comprised the prayer team.

Critical reading and initial corrections were provided by Lori Angel, Gary Arnone, Bev Carr, John Coyne, Paul DiMarco, Charles Galda Jr., Paul Hine, Dr. Jey Jeyapalan, Barbara Nelson, Joy Norman, Jennifer Ober, Karen Petersen, Bob Pious, Deb Priolo, Melissa Shaw, Steve Tanenbaum, and Joann Wright. I did not always agree with the corrections, so I cannot thank them enough for all the ways they made me reexamine the text.

Then to Trish Roccuzzo and my assistant, Leslie Goodwin, who typed, reshaped, retyped, and corrected all the corrections. To Bev Carr and Anna Mae Sholtes who tried to shape, adopt and move the material to a more coherent whole. To these I give my deep appreciation.

Then there are those who gave great practical support. Much of the book was written in the Dominican Republic; and Anja, with the staff at Lifestyle Holidays, did a great job encouraging and supporting me with help in many ways. And of course to Señor Alessandro, "Sandy," goes my thanks for cup after cup of coffee and for his attentiveness through early mornings of writing in the balcony restaurant overlooking the sea.

But . . . to my darling Ruth and to my colleagues on staff goes my gratitude for just "living with me" through the process. And I give thanks to the Lord who birthed a desire in me so many years ago—one that is reflected in these pages.

Finally, to Andy Sloan, the editor Authentic provided. I cannot thank you enough, Andy, for the tireless support and incredible abilities God has given you. Without you, I don't think this could have happened.

The final word of thanks goes to Clay Norman, the chairman of the Elder Board and my friend, who coordinated, encouraged, prayed, and believed in this.

To you all, one word: *eucharizomai.*

CHAPTER ONE

Hungry

THE DISAPPOINTED CHRISTIAN

D o you remember your excitement as a child when you crawled into bed Christmas Eve and wondered what the morning would bring? Over and over you imagined what it would feel like to unwrap that special gift! You could see the colors, you could feel the texture—it would finally be yours. Months of hints and suggestions would bring delight. The waiting was nearly complete; Christmas morning was almost here!

When you ran down the stairs and looked under the tree, you saw that special gift, which made you giggle as you danced around the tree. But perhaps it wasn't there, and you experienced disappointment when you expected joy. Your parents knew your hope but made a different choice based on their understanding—even though it was painful. A playful puppy might replace the dream of a pony, or a special dress might appear instead of the hoped-for playhouse. Perhaps a bicycle was leaning against the wall instead of a Nintendo.

Do you remember when your dreams didn't match what you received?

When I was a child I begged to go away to boarding school. My parents were kind and loving in trying to dissuade me from this desire, but the books I read painted it as a life of fun and excitement. I was warned that there was a gap between my mental image and the truth, but I felt I knew best. I should have listened. Boarding school failed to match my expectations and became a tremendous disappointment compared to what I had envisioned.

We often construct our own picture of what life should be and how it should turn out. We try to shape the path ahead. Sometimes our vision is fulfilled. But sometimes life doesn't turn out the way we hoped, and we may not know why.

Hungry for More

A young man met with me to discuss his spiritual life. He began by sharing about the failure of the local church to meet his needs. As we talked further, he revealed more of his heart's longing. "Surely there is more to this whole Christian thing!" He had recognized a basic tenet of the Christian life: it's not enough to live the same life as before we met Jesus, with Bible-reading, church, and praying added on.

At least once a month I talk to people who love Jesus but are disillusioned about their spiritual condition. They come to Christ to drink from the well of new life, yet their thirst remains.

This isn't what they expected, and their disappointment is obvious. They aren't rejecting what they were given, but they wonder, "Is this all that's available? Why didn't I get what I expected?"

Some blame themselves for lacking commitment and question whether their faith is really genuine. Others experience emptiness in their Christian life and wonder if that is normal. Some see advances in their professional or family life, but they cannot understand why there seems to be so little progress in their spiritual life. Terms like "stagnant" and "standing still" are used. Such awareness is uncomfortable. Why hasn't the Christian life met their expectations for spiritual growth, and how can they satisfy their craving for the Christian walk to have a deeper impact?

The nineteenth-century British novelist Charles Dickens told the sad story of a young orphan boy named Oliver Twist. Confined to the workhouse, Oliver is placed under the care of Mr. Bumble, an authoritarian taskmaster. Because the children are forced to work so hard and are fed so meagerly, they are perpetually hungry. Finally the children can stand the hunger no longer, and Oliver is selected to light the torch of revolt. He reluctantly approaches Mr. Bumble with his empty bowl to ask, with childlike innocence, about the possibility of getting more. The mere request is enough to throw the workhouse staff into panic. No one had ever possessed the courage to ask for more!

Do you sometimes in your spiritual life feel as Oliver felt? Do you want more from God? Are you hungry for a deeper relationship with him? If so, please read on.

Awakening

Summer in England may be a brief season, but a walk on a warm day in the wooded hills just outside London, as the sun sinks on the horizon, can turn your thoughts toward heaven. Many years ago, as a young preacher, I wandered on these hills late one afternoon. Although I was reflecting on heaven, my life at the time felt more like hell on earth. It had taken me a long time to become a Christian. Now, five years later, even though I had been ordained and was seeking to serve Jesus, it was proving hard to remain a Christian.

I desperately wanted Jesus to make me into a different kind of person. I knew where I *wanted* to go but felt impotent and frustrated in my efforts to arrive there. I had been promised the transforming power of Jesus, yet somehow it never materialized enough for me to really become different. I understood only too well the words of the apostle Paul, "What I want to do I do not do, but what I hate I do. . . . I have the desire to do what is good, but I cannot carry it out" (Romans 7:15, 18). This realization was beginning to tear me apart.

Frankly, my faith was head knowledge that had not really connected with my heart. If it had, then I would not have been so hungry for more.

Desperately Seeking the Real Thing

Walking alone that summer afternoon, I was comforted to remember that Jesus really is all he claimed to be. I found it reassuring to rehearse the evidence of my faith. Yet this remained just theory. There had to be more I could *experience* than I had discovered so far. I had tried different systems, programs, and ideas. I had searched the "higher Christian life," the "basic Christian life," and much in between. Still this seemed to feed only my mind. I was tired of sermons and spiritual thoughts; I longed to know God and was not satisfied with secondhand experience.

Then it hit me between the eyes as I sat on a grassy knoll reading a little book that had been recommended to me. Majestic words of the twentieth-century Chicago pastor A. W. Tozer came as a bolt from the blue:

> In this hour of all but universal darkness one cheering gleam appears: within the fold of conservative Christianity there are to be found increasing numbers of persons whose religious lives are marked by a growing hunger after God himself. They are eager for spiritual reality and will not be put off with words, nor will they be content with correct "interpretations" of truth. They are athirst for God, and they will not be satisfied till they have drunk deep at the fountain of living water. This is the only real harbinger of revival which I have been able to detect anywhere on the religious horizon. It may be the cloud the size of a man's hand for which a few saints here and there have been looking. It can result in a resurrection of life.[1]

---

1. A. W. Tozer, *The Pursuit of God* (Camp Hill, PA: Christian Publications, Inc., 1982), 8.

For the first time, I recognized the truth. I was looking for a resurrection in my Christian life. The only problem was that I hadn't foreseen that resurrection is necessarily preceded by *crucifixion*. There has to be a kind of death before one can be resurrected and enter into new life.

The truth was, all the time I had been looking in the wrong direction. I had been searching for something new to *add* to my spiritual life, but God wanted to *subtract* my intrusive will and replace it with his will. The prerequisite for God to work in my life and to renew it was that I willingly lay down my life. No two individuals can be masters in a house at the same time. In the same way, two competing priorities cannot be held by one person without creating spiritual schizophrenia. When God lives his life in us there is no room for two independent spirits. One must submit to the other.

As the wind ruffled the grass around me, I knelt in humble appreciation that Jesus did not come just to *teach* me how to live—he wanted to *show* me how to live. He showed us how to die and that death would come through a cross. There he revealed the secret of the "crucified life."

Life Begins at the Cross

That day on the hill I learned that the Christian life does not grow by acquisition from God, but rather by surrender to him. I cannot receive all that he longs to give me until I first make room for him to work in my life. Resurrection follows crucifixion. It dawned on me that Jesus' death on the cross achieved two things: how to die, and how to live. The cross didn't mark the end; instead, it marked a new beginning for all who would be introduced to a crucified life. God desires our unqualified devotion. Crucified love is his gift to us. Resurrected life with God is his purpose. He requires that we, too, live a crucified life.

Such a life is surrendered—sacrificed to Jesus and broken of self-will. It is dead to our own desires and lives for his glory rather than our own. That is the life of a disciple: our power exchanged for his, making us fulfilled and fruitful. A crucified life realizes the dreams and hopes laid before us in God's Word and energized by the Holy Spirit.

This truth poses a major problem for many of us. For far too long we have been presented with a version of the Christian faith that majors on what we get rather than on what we give. The cross has been portrayed as the place where Jesus died for us and where we receive from him, but rarely is it shown as the location of our joint crucifixion with Christ.

The uncomfortable truth is that Jesus calls us to share his cross. He said that "anyone who does not take his cross and follow me is not worthy of me" (Matthew 10:38). Jesus explained that he was not going to do all the dying so we could comfortably enjoy all the living. He insisted, on the contrary: "If anyone would come after me, he must deny himself and take up his cross and follow me" (Matthew 16:24). This rigorous challenge comes at the beginning of faith, not halfway along the journey.

We have become accustomed to Christian literature that outlines programs and processes for changing our lives so that we may benefit more from living for Jesus. This was never what Jesus intended. His purpose was not to call us to a glib "easy-believism." Instead, he challenged people to come and die, a death that was not intended to be an end, but a beginning. This explains the words of Jesus, "Whoever finds his life will lose it, and whoever loses his life for my sake will find it" (Matthew 10:39). Instead of using self-discipline and hard work to conform our will to God's will, we can live by his power and life within us.

So how do I live the crucified life? It all begins at the cross. There I abandon control of my own life and surrender it into the hands of the one who died for me. Then I stop trying to live for Jesus and start allowing him to live his life through me. This is the crucified life. Perhaps this does not seem attractive, sounding too much like hard work. Actually the opposite is true, for the wonder of it all is that through a crucified *death* Jesus offers the only doorway to resurrection and to a crucified *life*. As I die to myself, Jesus creates new life in me and through me. He begins to exchange my energies, desires, abilities, and passions for his! This is a whole new life, one that starts with a cross.

Dying to Live

At first glance this appears to be a contradiction. Here, however, is the supreme paradox. For how can life emerge from death? How can a person die and live simultaneously? How can the suffering and disgrace of the cross ever be regarded as something with a wonderful outcome?

On that sun-dappled afternoon in England, I first glimpsed the understanding that Jesus does not require my best effort. Instead, he wants to live *his* life in *me*. He doesn't want to improve the old version; he wants to *replace* it. When I came to that realization, my world exploded. No longer did I search for textbooks on how to live. I had discovered the great, liberating truth that Jesus simply wanted to live *through* me.

As I stood, brushed off the grass, and left the hillside behind, I could scarcely believe what I had discovered. I saw the landscape of my life in a new light. The Christian life was not a teller's counter from which to withdraw gifts from the bank of heaven for my own benefit. No, this was the place to invest my life, for God's glory.

It was becoming clear that Jesus' death on the cross had achieved two things: it showed me the way to live, and it showed me the way to die. This meant that I could start to live through Jesus' life within rather than work on self-improvements in my old life. I could exchange his life for mine.

Luis Palau, the Argentinean-born evangelist, has spoken about the deep discouragement he felt early in his relationship with God. He recalls how one day as a young man he was reduced to feeling "fit to quit." He felt inadequate for the challenge God had given him to go and change the world. He knew he lacked the required personal resources. The awareness of this inadequacy did not prove to be solely negative for Luis. Far from it! This realization proved to be the doorway to a deep surrender that would transform him into a man God could use to touch hundreds of thousands of people.

When we stop trying to prove or to improve ourselves, God can step into our lives in a fresh way. When we allow the Lord to reduce us to a position where we too are "fit to quit," then he can do a deeper work in our hearts and lives. When we stop searching for ways to change ourselves, we prepare for a journey of discovery into all that *he has for us*—not what *we have for him.*

The death of our old nature must precede new life. This is not, of course, about taking our lives physically. Instead, we surrender our inner nature and priorities for a higher purpose. In essence we die to ourselves in order that we might live for God. We follow the instruction of a father who sacrificed his son and who desires that we lose our lives so that we may find them again.

As Paul phrased it for the early church, "Don't you know that all of us who were baptized into Christ Jesus were baptized into his death? We were therefore buried with him through baptism into death in order that, just as Christ was raised from the dead through the glory of the Father, we too may live a new life" (Romans 6:3–4).

Only the life of the risen Lord Jesus vividly displayed in you and in me will make a difference. We may *want* to change. We may even *expect* to create godly change within ourselves. True change, however, will never result from our human efforts.

Beyond the Cross

How do dying and living embrace each other in the "crucified life"? How does the paradox become resolved? Like a valuable gemstone, the Christian life has various facets. Each chapter of this book deals with one facet.

- **Crucified**—I view my life from a cross. I offer my spirit and inner nature to be renewed by the one who first gave me life.

- **Surrender**—I abdicate the throne of my life to Jesus' reign and rule.
- **Disciple**—I follow the only leader worthy of my devotion and service.
- **Sacrifice**—I gamble my life, but not with dice. I risk my life for God's purposes.
- **Giving**—I lose my priority of self-interest for service to others.
- **Exchange**—I transfer my life to Jesus, exchanging it for his life in me.
- **Dying**—I die to myself so that Jesus can enable me to live for him.
- **Broken**—I pour out my life and love in appreciation for the love given to me.
- **Spirit-Filled**—I know that God himself lives in me, and I experience the glorious roller-coaster ride of life in the Spirit.
- **Fruit**—I live a transformed life that is productive and gives me the excitement of seeing results in my Christian walk.
- **Destiny**—I receive life from God not to waste it, but to live for a purpose—a glorious purpose!

In all of these facets Christ speaks. He offers life from a cross for me to share: a *crucified life*, the only antidote to the "do-it-yourself" religion I tried for so long.

You could say that my friend Ted was born with a guitar in his hands. His passion to play music was reflected in a career of clubs, bands, and solo performances, punctuated by the occasional steady job and paycheck when things got desperate. He desired musical excellence, and as a result he had a successful career as a professional musician. Despite success in his career, Ted experienced sickness in his family, rejection at work, and the disappointment of unfulfilled musical dreams that brought him as low as he had ever been.

It was then that Ted faced the cross of Jesus. He found, to his surprise, that Jesus hadn't died simply to bring him the good life he wanted. Instead, Christ asked Ted to join him! A joint crucifixion was not the life Ted had anticipated. Nor were his problems disappearing. He continued to need God's strength and care, but his life was starting to change.

The men's ministry at church needed a worship leader, so Ted reluctantly stepped into the role. Looking back, he recalls, "We sounded nothing like the professional, album-cutting worship team I envisioned." He wanted to leave his post, but the Lord reminded him that a crucified life does not act on its own desires. It cannot—it is anchored to a cross.

Ted humbled himself, as Jesus did on the cross. Today, the Lord reveals himself through Ted's music ministry; and Ted is glad he chose to remain a worship leader. Others recognize that his life has changed, and Ted is experiencing true inner joy. He still reminds himself, "It isn't about me and my musical ability; it is about God and his glory."

In dying to live, we are introduced to the joy of resurrection.

Prayer ▶ Lord Jesus, it is incredible that you not only died *for* me but you also expect me to share in that death. And thank you, Lord, that it does not end there. Please help me to relax in your love and allow you to live your life through me. Introduce me to the joy of knowing and living a crucified life. Amen.

CHAPTER TWO

Crucified

THE CRUCIFIED LIFE

The young preacher looked uncertain. His voice quivered slightly, his knees trembled, and his palms were soaked. He intended to recite a quotation, but he couldn't remember its source. His eyes anxiously scanned his notes to discover the author's identity. A long pause . . . Ah! He had it. "Yes, J. Mighal . . . Smith." Sympathetic laughter rippled through the congregation. To forget such a common surname!

Struggling on, the preacher read the apostle Paul's words in 2 Timothy 2:11–12: "If we died with him, we will also live with him; if we endure, we will also reign with him." He moved into familiar territory as he shared, "If a seed dies, then the plant will live. If a bulb is buried in the earth, then the flower can grow. Dying has to come before living."

As conviction mounted, his words intensified. This truth was the all-consuming passion of his heart, an unusual conviction to be held so deeply by a young man just starting his ministry. As he poured out his soul, he sensed that God himself had rooted those words deep within him—and God would not miss the mark!

Living Away from the Cross

If you guessed that I was that young preacher, you are correct! Looking back, thirty-five years later, I am left with one relentless question: Where did that message go? The message never completely disappeared; there were occasions when I vividly preached the cross. But there were just so many other messages upon which a young preacher could dwell. When I did preach about the cross, the focus was Jesus dying for me—rarely was the idea me dying with him!

During the past fifty or so years, an emphasis on the crucified life has drifted to the background of Christian thought. Some have almost taken the concept for granted because it has been a vital part of their Christian walk for so long. But we need to ask, "Have we passed the message on?"

Quietly and unobtrusively, the issue of our dying has been overtaken by what we regard as more important matters of life. A whole generation has grown up on a diet of the latest programs and processes (for example, "Use this five-point plan to achieve a victorious walk"). We explore new strategies to impact society with the love of Jesus. We seek more relevance in our church programs. We try to find deeper insights and greater vitality to communicate Christ to those who have never encountered him. But after trying our best, we may sense that an aching hunger remains—a lingering desire for more of God in our lives. It's not uncommon today to hear that people are searching for fresh reservoirs of the Spirit's power.

As I examine the myriad of Christian books written in the past fifty years on every subject under the sun, I encounter a great omission. The error is fundamental, and I admit that I am among those who failed to notice. Influenced by the tide of Christian opinion, I failed to remember that the heart of Christian faith lies first in a cross and then in an empty tomb. Crucifixion precedes resurrection.

My call from God was to preach the crucified life. I have neglected that call at my own peril.

God calling his people to live on the far side of the cross. Jesus' death on the cross was not simply what God did for us in the past, but it's also what God wants for each one of us now. But don't misunderstand! The cross of Jesus Christ *does* represent a once-and-for-all event. His death encompassed all dying, opened salvation to all, and obliterated the power of death. No action on our part can support or complement what Jesus has done. His death stands alone.

Do we also have a cross? Jesus said, "Anyone who does not carry his cross and follow me cannot be my disciple" (Luke 14:27). Notice the important wording: "*his* cross." Jesus was referring to *every* person. The supreme test of discipleship that Jesus imposed on his followers is that each one should be ready to "give up everything he has" (Luke 14:33) and then "deny himself and take up his cross and follow me" (Matthew 16:24). The idea of sharing in Christ's crucifixion is never comfortable.

What is this cross that is reserved for us? The words of the twentieth-century prophet A. W. Tozer have been very helpful to me. "It is not a cross on a hill nor a cross on a church. It is not a cross that can be worn around the neck. It must be the cross of obedience to the will of God, and we must embrace it, each believer for himself."[1]

When obedience is not a single event but a *daily* experience, then we walk voluntarily in the footsteps of our Lord Jesus. The result is what Paul calls the "trustworthy saying," that "If we died with him, we will also live with him" (2 Timothy 2:11). As Paul assured the church at Colosse, "You died, and your life is now hidden with Christ in God" (Colossians 3:3).

As we live secure in this reality, we can sense our partnership with Jesus in building the kingdom of God and know that those who endure unrestricted crucifixion can anticipate resurrection in his glory. That's the wonderful paradox of the crucified life!

Living Where Christ Reigns

Phil and Becca Smith knew comfort and security because of Phil's executive position in a leading American corporation. Then God intruded into their comfortable, secure lives. First, Phil was called to serve as executive pastor of their home church, where we worked together in happy collaboration. Today, they serve alongside churches in troubled, post-genocide Rwanda

---

1. A. W. Tozer, *The Radical Cross* (Camp Hill, PA: Wing Spread Publishers, 2006), 77.

as country directors for World Relief, ministering to the poor, to those living with HIV/AIDS, and to displaced widows and orphans.

Recently Phil and Becca visited our church. It's always fun to be reunited with them, and I took the opportunity to interview them during the weekend services. I have a slight mischievous streak, so during our conversation in front of the congregation, I offered Phil his old job. I knew what his response would be. "Look, I would love to," he said. "But God has called us to be where we are in Rwanda. We want to obey him."

God challenges each of us to live for him, wherever we are. Whether in your hometown or city, within your homeland or overseas, in safety or danger—whatever the circumstances—God wants to live in and through you.

For each person who has surrendered his or her life to Jesus Christ there exists two corresponding biblical symbols: a cross and a throne. Our natural inclination is to concentrate all attention on achieving the throne and to forget that the cross comes first. The apostle Paul was not reluctant to face this truth. He reminded the Christians in Colosse that they "died with Christ to the basic principles of this world" (Colossians 2:20), and he warned the believers in Rome that one day they would be held accountable for the way they had lived (Romans 14:10–12).

We may prefer to anticipate the throne, but the only way to get there is by way of the cross. The route always includes conflict, which Jesus experienced in the garden of Gethsemane, between our will and that of Father God. His will must triumph in our lives for the way to the throne, via the cross, to be secured.

Our selfish will can be so stubborn and proud. It always seeks to guard its own rights rather than capitulate to the will of God. We defend ourselves strongly against any attack from others or any attempt by God to show us the truth about ourselves. We get angry, envious, and anxious. We find fault with others and resist giving in. Even if we try to do everything correctly, we can do it in the wrong spirit or with the wrong motives. Our flesh will even try to do God's work, but the results will not be effective. That is why the flesh has to be crucified—it cannot simply be changed.

We need to abdicate the throne of our life so that Jesus can reign. As long as we concentrate on *our* throne, we will remain the king of our own tiny kingdom. Only when we allow Christ to bring us to our cross will anything change. *If we refuse the cross of obedience, then we remain on a fruitless throne.*

Living in an Upside-Down Kingdom

No one chooses the cross—until desperate to have all that God would do in us. We each must die on our own cross, not on one belonging to someone else. Then we sacrifice everything to his will in serving Jesus Christ. It isn't about *part of our life* being crucified with Christ, but *all of life* being offered to God. Here we discover the difference between a life of growing sainthood and one of spiritual mediocrity. Some are content to stop halfway on their climb up the mountain, while others are determined not to stop short of finishing the ascent with Jesus.

Look closely and see that the apostle Paul does not say "Jesus Christ was crucified for me, I have only to receive the benefits."

Instead, he announces no less than a joint crucifixion: "I have been crucified with Christ and I no longer live, but Christ lives in me" (Galatians 2:20). He gives no suggestion that this is a deluxe type of Christian experience. Paul is describing the reality of the normal Christian life. This is what transformed him to live an incredible life. Being crucified was an ongoing reality in his daily experience.

Let us turn again to the words of Tozer:

> Though the cross of Christ has been beautified by the poet and the artist, the person avidly seeking God will likely experience it as the same savage implement of destruction it was in the days of old. The way of the cross is still the pain-wracked path to spiritual power and fruitfulness.
>
> So do not seek to hide from it. Do not accept an easy way. Do not allow yourself to be patted to sleep in a comfortable church, void of power and barren of fruit. Do not paint the cross nor deck it with flowers. Take it for what it is, as it is, and you will find it the rugged way to death and life. Let it slay you utterly.[2]

While writing these words, I met Pastor Jim. Until recently he supported his family with a well-paying job at a cement company in Illinois. A small, struggling church of fifty people needed a pastor, and Jim was God's man for the job. There is no amazing end to this story. The congregation remains about the same size. Life is not significantly easier for Jim or for his

---

2. Ibid., 66.

family. Much has been surrendered, and many sacrifices have been made. Pastor Jim does not see these as reasons to return to his former position. That is the crucified life: the day-by-day dedication of all we have and are to God's purposes for our life.

What does this mean? It reveals that to live you must first die to yourself; and when you die, you begin to live a vibrant, eternal life. The Christian starts to learn that the crucified life is God's introduction to his upside-down kingdom. And here the paradox becomes still more obvious. In the upside-down kingdom, you

- Are strongest when you are weak.
- Are rich when what you have is at the Lord's disposal, but you are poor when retaining control of wealth.
- Sin less when conscious of sin, but you are vulnerable when feeling invincible.
- Are most ready for heaven when serving God's business on earth, but you are least ready for eternal glory when serving your own interests.

It all boils down to realizing that our security, well-being, and fruitfulness lie in Christ, not in our own performance. Paul wrote of this life-transforming condition in these words: "May I never boast except in the cross of our Lord Jesus Christ, through which the world has been crucified to me, and I to the world" (Galatians 6:14).

This is not the culmination, but the beginning of new things our God wants to do in us and through us.

Living God's Way

Is this life too extreme? It can seem so to us. But the Lord Jesus always mades exclusive claims on the lives of his disciples. Rather than adopting a lifestyle of "Jesus . . . and something else," we are pointed to the way of "Jesus . . . and *nothing* else!" Jesus said that anyone wanting to follow him without loving him more than anything or anyone, father and mother, wife and children, brothers and sisters—even his own life—that person could not be his disciple (Luke 14:26). Even those things we hold most dear are to be relegated to second place.

Consider how Jacob and his twin brother, Esau, differed in their responses to God's love and grace. Esau typifies a self-made man. He threw away his birthright for a bowl of soup (Genesis 25:29–34), which is why Scripture says God rejected him (Malachi 1:1–4; Hebrews 12:16–17). Esau was a man like the nineteenth-century British prime minister, Benjamin Disraeli, famous for his ego and self-assertiveness as a political opponent. John Bright said of Disraeli, "He is a self-created man, and he worships his creator."

Self-dependency results in a character that excludes any need for God. In fact, God can do nothing with the person who stubbornly refuses to admit that he or she needs anything from God. When it came to "real life," Esau saw little place for God. Esau knew,

> It matters not how straight the gate,
> How charged with punishment the scroll,
> I am the master of my fate:
> I am the captain of my soul.
>
> ("Invictus," by William Henley)

At first reading this might sound like the stuff of great novels: a practical man or woman governed by self-confidence and a strategic plan of action. But to God it sounds the death knell to a life of useful service.

Esau's brother, Jacob, was devious and manipulative, a liar and a cheat. Surely God could not make anything useful of this man! If we could choose one of these men for a neighbor, straightforward Esau would be preferred to scheming Jacob. Yet the Lord recognized the potential within Jacob to become someone much more effective in the kingdom of God. Under the surface God saw a person who could passionately love and serve him.

In Genesis 32 the Lord wrestled with Jacob; and Jacob clung to God until he received a blessing. Then God changed his name from Jacob, which means "deceiver," to Israel, which means "one who has struggled with God." During their struggle the Lord wrenched Jacob's hip out of joint. This man would walk with a limp for the rest of his life as a constant reminder of the one who was now in control. The only hope for Jacob, this master of deception, lay in his being conquered. God defeated Jacob so that he might become a new man. Talk about a paradox!

God looks at us with a similar gaze—not only seeing what we are but also all that we can become. That is what he wants to do for us. Stubborn, self-willed, rebellious Jacob/Israel always had a limp to remind him that he was on the road to becoming a useful and dignified friend of God. That is the way of the cross. *It destroys confidence in our fleshly abilities and renders us totally dependent on the power of God's Spirit.*

Only when we have been conquered can we truly be blessed. Only then will we know the joys and triumphs as well as the pain of a crucified life. Only then will we walk with a limp so others will know that we have been mastered by God. Such a state is rarely rewarded with popular accolades or much fanfare. Our lives may not appear to produce spectacular results, but our rewards remain a gift from God, whose cross we can now share. This path is not reserved for great apostles, such as Peter and Paul. It is the same path that humble pilgrims today can follow.

I think of Hubert and Junie Morquette. Both are natives of Haiti, a nation considered to be third-world within its region and the HIV/AIDS capital of the Caribbean. Hubert and Junie graduated as medical doctors and surgeons from the historic University of Paris. They had the world at their feet. But they laid prestige, power, finances, and friendship aside to do what God told them to do.

As an aside, we often think of those who leave friends, family, and their country as the only "heroes" for Jesus. No doubt, there is heroism in those who follow God's call to sacrifice the familiar for an unknown life far away. Yet there is also a quiet heroism in staying where God has planted you, which can also be a sacrifice, and patiently serving God with little recognition for the life you have laid down for him.

Consider again the husband and wife physicians. Unknown to the rest of the world, they can still be found in Haiti—serving God, healing their people, living the crucified life, and rejecting the glittering prizes that would otherwise be theirs. They know there will be plenty of time to receive heaven's greater rewards. To thousands of sick children, poverty-stricken widows, AIDS sufferers, and people with unfulfilled potential, this crucified man and woman bring hope, a future, and the love of Jesus.

Prayer ▶ Lord, it seems such a contradiction that you want me to live a crucified life so that I may know the joy of your resurrection power. I'm not even sure that I know what that will mean for me, but I want more of your empowerment in my life—whatever the consequences. Please help me to continually take up my cross, and fill me daily with your new life. Amen.

CHAPTER THREE

Surrender

THE ART OF STARTING OVER

My children always called him Mikey-Moo. It was their affectionate nickname for our family friend who, with his wife Katey, lived just around the corner as our kids were growing up. When Mike enrolled as a history student at Oxford University, he had no idea that he would meet Jesus and dedicate his future to him. When I met Mike, he had been a Christian for just three months.

I have watched Mike walk through life. In my role as pastor, I married Mike and Katey and saw them enter a life of Christian ministry. I remember praying with them that their lives might become emptied of themselves and filled with the Holy Spirit. This was a time of joy and excitement, brimming with anticipation for all that the future would hold for the two of them.

Mike was dedicated in his work for the Lord: first as the administrator who launched Spring Harvest, the largest Christian festival in Europe; next as the advocate who established the Religious Liberty Commission of the World Evangelical Fellowship; and then as an entrepreneur who established, guided, motivated, and supported many individuals and ministries. My affable, warm, genial, and sometimes eccentric friend—who comes about as close to being a genius as anyone I know—really made an impact in the service of his Lord.

My wife, Ruth, and I have also walked with Mike and Katey in the midst of some great disappointments. They felt anguish as they dealt with infertility and the realization that they would not have their own children. Later, when we were on vacation with them in France, Katey stumbled during a walk. Shortly thereafter multiple sclerosis began to loom large in their lives. We watched the virulence of the disease destroy first Katey's body, then her memory. I witnessed Mike's compassion through years of nursing his wife, until doing so was no longer possible.

I know this man well. Mike embodies the reality of a relationship with Jesus. I sense that the person I knew as a student at Oxford University is not the same one I know now. Beyond his initial decision to follow Christ, Mike absolutely understands what it means to live a crucified life, and—as he visits Katey in a nursing home—he is readily able to describe the meaning of this experience.

Mike doesn't agree with the idea that Jesus intends for us to enjoy a life of undisturbed comfort and success. He is amused by TV evangelists who assure that one only needs more faith in order to have a wonderful life.

While walking with God, has Mike made mistakes and faltered at times? Yes. But he kept going, and each step brought lessons from God that deepened him along his journey. Because of this, Mike has survived tremendous pain with a spirit of joy. This is no mere human effort. It is a perseverance that is divine in origin; it comes as a gift from the Holy Spirit; it is an inner fortitude that springs from a long walk with God.

The idea of a shared crucifixion makes sense to Mike. The Savior who died for him now calls him to a crucified life, where each moment of crucifixion introduces a new instance of resurrection. You see, the life of faith does not stop when you meet Jesus—that is when it begins.

An Ongoing Relationship

We might refer to the moment we began our relationship with Jesus in a way that sounds like the culmination of our previous life rather than the beginning of our new life. Placing too much stress on our initiation to faith makes the *introduction* appear to be the whole story. Paul's blazing moment of revelation on the Damascus road (Acts 9:5) happened perhaps eight years before he and Barnabas formed a ministry team together. These were eight years of patient discipleship as God shaped Paul's inner nature.

Think of a marriage. Those of us with married children, especially daughters, know about "wedding fever." A staggering amount of money can be spent to support this one life-changing day! You learn enough about bridesmaids' dresses, invitations, photographs, speeches, rehearsals, and receptions to last a lifetime. There is reason, of course, to celebrate and remember. But though the wedding is important, it marks only the beginning; life together will become the real marriage.

Some people live their Christian life based on their recollection of how it first began. If we are married we need to pay attention to what our relationship is like now rather than resting on the memory of the wedding day. How long can a marriage remain vibrant if it consists only of wedding reminiscences and photographs? When we become Christians, we enter an eternal marriage. If we rely only on the moment we come to faith, we miss the ongoing richness of the relationship. True conversion is the doorway to lifelong discipleship. Both are essential.

The English preacher and author John Stott has stressed that we need to know that Christianity is more than a one-time experience—it is ongoing. He has often said, "I have been saved, I am being saved, and I am going to be saved." Stott admits that this emphasis didn't originate with him. When preaching at the 1979 Urbana Convention he said, "I am myself always grateful to the good man who led me to Christ over forty years ago that he taught me, raw and brash convert that I was, to keep saying: 'I have been saved (in the past) from the penalty of sin by a crucified Savior. I am being saved (in the present) from the power of sin by a living Savior. And I shall be saved (in the future) from the very presence of sin by a coming Savior.'"[1]

---

1. John Stott, "The Messenger and God, Part 4: God's People (Romans 5:1–11)" sermon at 1979 Urbana Convention, Urbana-Champaign, IL,

Starting Over

If you want to start a new life, there is no better place to begin than with Jesus. "In him was life, and that life was the light of men" (John 1:4). Jesus told a religious leader that he needed to start life afresh. He needed to be "born again" (John 3:3). But there is more: "Whoever claims to live in him must walk as Jesus did" (1 John 2:6).

Jesus arrived at the shore of the Sea of Galilee and called some fishermen to follow him (Matthew 4:18–22; Luke 5:1–11). While the call took only a moment, Jesus then invested three years teaching these men and showing them how to live their lives in a radically different way.

Consider these two questions:

- What was the starting point of their journey? They left their boats and nets.
- What came next? They started to *follow Jesus.*

What does it mean for us today when we respond to God's call? Some suggest that our response to Jesus is only that we "accept" him. This is a very different message than the call to be "born again," which is entering into a personal relationship with Jesus Christ. Do we control the time, place, circumstances, and conditions of becoming a Christian? No! How we come to Christ never depends on our preferences, but rather it depends on his leading. Scripture calls us "servants" of Jesus (Romans 1:1) and "slaves" of God (Romans 6:22). Slaves don't negotiate

---

http://www.urbana.org/_articles.cfm?RecordId=1088.

a contract with their master; they simply obey their master's instructions.

The question is not "Will the sinner accept the Savior?" but "Will the Savior accept the sinner?" The idea of "accepting Jesus as Savior" is not reflected in any Bible verse. Instead, throughout Scripture God reiterates that he will welcome us to himself. We are to respond to his love and reject all other alternatives.

Words can convey different meanings to different generations. The connotation behind the phrases "accepting Jesus" and "receiving Christ" can convey far more than the words themselves. Faithful, sincere preachers have adopted these phrases because of the emphasis placed on God's initiative and grace. Many of us have been steeped in this language and have begun genuine journeys of faith as a result of it. However, in an increasingly secular world the notion of "accepting" Jesus tends to communicate cheap grace and a casual attitude toward the Christian life. Crucified love demands much more from us. While most believers who use these terms acknowledge that coming to Christ entails sacrificing ourselves to him and for him, our words need to convey that truth clearly.

The idea of "accepting Jesus" may have successfully launched many of us on our spiritual journey. But the phrase itself sounds a little patronizing, for we are not doing God a favor by offering him partnership in our lives. Phrases like "committing our lives to Jesus" or "surrendering control of our lives to Christ" more closely conveys what we mean to a twenty-first century world.

We can never hope to welcome the King of kings, the Lord of lords, the one and only Son of God into our lives on our terms. If Jesus is our Savior, then he must also live and reign in us as Lord of every area of our lives. The words we choose must make that demand obvious and explicit. Jesus gave his life for us, and he requires the same of us in return.

Too Much "Easy-Believism"

When an earthquake caused a jailer in Philippi to ask the critical question, "What must I do to be saved?" the apostle Paul's reply was brief and to the point: "Believe in the Lord Jesus, and you will be saved" (Acts 16:30–31). Did Paul mean then what we would understand from that statement today? Probably not. But Paul and Silas didn't leave it at that. The jailer took them to his home, and they "spoke the word of the Lord to him and to all the others in his house" (Acts 16:32). Only after that further explanation was the jailer, and his family, baptized (Acts 16:33–34). Surely hearing more than "Believe in the Lord Jesus" was necessary, particularly if they had never before heard of Jesus. And Paul and Silas certainly would have noted the significance—and the cost—of the action these people were taking. After all, this same Paul insisted that baptism is a sign of dying to ourselves that we might live for God (Romans 6:3–4).

My father was a Christian. Many years ago I asked him this question: "What does *believe* mean to you as a member of your generation?" He replied, "It means a total and complete surrender of your life to Jesus Christ, recognizing that he died because he loves you, and asking him to share his life with

you by living in you as your Lord and Savior." The Greek verb
we translate as "believe," *pisteuo*, has precisely that meaning!
Implying more than mere rational agreement, it includes
a sense of trust arising from a personal relationship. This
meaning is reflected in the New Testament, since the verb is
commonly followed by a preposition: "believe *in*."

Unfortunately, for many the word *believe* may only indicate
that someone has a basic recognition of certain truths. It can
convey an intellectual acceptance rather than a radical commitment to a changed lifestyle. The devil believes there is a God,
and he cannot deny the existence of Jesus; but that hardly quali-
fies Satan to be called a "believer" or a "Christian!" We have so
simplified the meaning of the words *believe* and *belief* that one
could conclude that head knowledge equals conversion! Viewed
that way, no radical change in lifestyle or perspective would be
required.

However, that is not God's perspective as revealed in the
Bible. The writers of the New Testament clearly understood that
the call to believe was also a call to discipleship. Nowhere is this
more pronounced than in Jesus' teaching. Time and again he
declared the need for his followers to deny themselves and take
up their cross. This clearly spells out the terms and conditions for
us to find new life in Jesus. These conditions are nonnegotiable
for a relationship with Christ, and they include the cost of daily
crucifying our old life and resurrecting into a new way of living.
Jesus offers no simple, prepackaged belief system to buy into,
no mere easygoing acceptance. As he starkly said, "Anyone who

does not carry his cross and follow me cannot be my disciple"
(Luke 14:27).

Complete Surrender

At the beginning of the nineteenth century, the British
admiral Lord Nelson defeated a French captain in a naval battle.
The captain boarded Nelson's ship to surrender, expecting to be
offered sympathetic condolences and a glass of wine. But, before
the hospitality could begin, he was greeted with a demand for his
sword. The captain was asked to demonstrate his willingness to
give up the fight and surrender the battle to Lord Nelson.

Jesus asks us for complete surrender to his will and purpose
for our lives. How do I live out this attitude of surrender? Is
it just a matter of adopting a regimen of spiritual disciplines?
No, the crucified life is far more than that! It is all-consuming,
all-transforming, and totally different. It involves both giving
and receiving. First I must surrender to God total control of my
life—two kings cannot reign alongside each other. My requirements are a broken spirit, contrite heart, and an emptying of my
ambitions so that he can bring his life into me and live through
me.

Jesus calls people not to "accept" him, gain a blessing, join
a club, or even acknowledge who he is. Instead, he calls us to go
further and follow him.

True belief is easy to identify. When it is in place, you will:

- Open your life to Jesus in simple trust and
  commitment.
- Surrender control and authority of your life to Jesus.

- Obey Jesus in every area of your life.
- Respond to Jesus' guidance with a life of active discipleship.
- Fall more and more in love with Jesus.

The call to discipleship represents a call to self-denial. As many people like Mike have discovered, the reality of giving way to Christ and giving in to Christ is a lifelong journey. Instead of expanding our own ambitions and desires—or expecting God to further them for us—we are called to surrender all that we have and are to the Lord Jesus. *We are called to trust him.*

Relaxing into Jesus

The first spiritual discipline Jesus modeled was submission. Jesus submitted to his Father, living a life of surrender to his will. Charles Swindoll points out, "As our example, Jesus modeled trust in the Father. He came to the planet that he had made and lived his entire life misunderstood, misrepresented, misquoted, mistreated and finally crucified. Yet he committed no sin. From Bethlehem's manger to Golgotha's cross, Jesus exemplified a life of surrender."[2] Trust in God is necessary in surrendering to him total control of our lives.

What does it mean to trust someone? I illustrated the concept during one of my sermons when I asked Tom—a builder in my congregation—to join me at the front of the church. I had Tom turn his back to me. Then I asked, "Tom, do you trust

---

2. Charles Swindoll, *So You Want to Be Like Christ?* (Nashville: Thomas Nelson, 2005), 86.

me?" and I told him to relax and fall backwards into my arms. The floor was hard, so it would hurt if I didn't catch him; and everyone would be watching if he made a fool of himself. There was a moment of silence, and then Tom just relaxed into my arms.

Jesus likewise calls us to trust him—both when things go well and when they fall apart. Look at how Jesus established his trustworthiness as he loved the unlovely, obeyed his Father, and instructed his followers. Through his life on earth he taught us how to trust him with our possessions, our positions, our plans, and our families.

Our natural self is programmed for self-preservation. It is an incredible challenge for us to surrender our health, marriage, reputation, ministry, friends, routine, and independence. These things define us. But they are all gifts from the Father. We need to discipline ourselves to hold them loosely (and with gratitude) and to not love them more than the one who gives "every good and perfect gift" (James 1:17).

Matt, an eighteen-year-old neighbor of mine, was running late as he pulled his car out of his driveway. He was on his way to witness his best friend's baptism, a special event that Matt didn't want to miss. Driving too fast, he lost control of the car as it slid off the road and flipped over into a stream. When the car came to a stop, Matt was hanging upside down and unable to escape, despite his significant efforts.

Suspended there, helpless and with time to think, Matt admits it wasn't a good time. But he quickly adds, "I wouldn't have missed it for anything!" In those moments of utter helplessness

Matt realized he had already handed control of his life over to Jesus. Someone else was with him in his predicament. Matt's life relaxed into the life of another, one who had rescued him even before the rescuers arrived.

This relationship of loving surrender and trust does not diminish us. Instead, it offers us the security of knowing that the King of kings, the creator of the universe, is living in us. Without that attitude of surrender we could never discover the life of adventure that God intends for those who entrust their destiny to him. Beginning with our initial surrender—and continuing until our final entry into eternity with him—surrender does not mean captivity, but freedom. It means we will never walk alone.

Prayer ▶ Lord, may I see you more clearly, love you more dearly, and follow you more nearly, day by day. Teach me to listen for your guidance and to ask for it in the details of my daily life. I give you permission to shape my inner being so that my desires are increasingly those of your heart. Please take all that I am, and enable me to become all that I can be as I relax into your love, life, and will. Amen.

CHAPTER FOUR

Disciple

SOLD OUT

My son Gavin is tall and strong. But since he doesn't have the slender build of a typical distance runner, our family was a little taken aback when Gavin announced that he was going to run a marathon to raise money for charity. No one questioned, however, whether he would complete the race. If Gavin decides to do something, he will train and prepare for it. Then, in the words of the famous Nike ad, he will "just do it." Once we knew of his determination to run a marathon, we would have been really surprised if he had dropped out before reaching the finish line.

"He nearly made it." "She almost did it." I think these are among the saddest words one can hear. I have always feared hearing a final verdict such as "You nearly made it, but you never quite managed to fulfill your potential." This verdict suits those who begin well but fail to keep going—even some whom we respect as spiritual leaders.

Time and again, men and women of God who started out well have ended their service for the Lord with shattered dreams and personal disappointment. This may have happened because of their failing to become all they longed to be in Jesus, because of their inability to cope with situations they faced, or even because of a moral or ethical collapse totally inconsistent with their spiritual calling. Whatever happened, they now look back with regret at what might have been.

If we want to complete our journey well, without the disappointment of *nearly* making it, then the only way to go is to the cross. A. W. Tozer once concluded that for a crucified man, whether he attains great sainthood or spiritual mediocrity depends upon which choice he makes.[1]

A Matter of the Will

We can have everything imaginable; but without the cross, one pitfall or another will trap us. Without the cross, you and I could know the disappointment of recognizing that we never quite made it. Fortunately, God knows where we are, and the grace of his crucified love is always drawing us to himself. He moves upon us in his own timing and initiative to call us to the great adventure of faith. His way is as unique in our lives as our own fingerprints. He waits until we are ready to surrender and prepared to rely on him.

---

1. A. W. Tozer, *The Radical Cross* (Camp Hill, PA: Wing Spread Publishers, 2006), 47.

Ravi Zacharias has observed, "Where does one begin? With self-crucifixion? In effect, we go to our own funeral and bury the self-will so that God's will can reign supremely in our hearts. Our will has no power to do God's will until it first dies to its own desires and the Holy Spirit brings a fresh power within."[2]

There is one thing that is safe about a cross. You can rely on the fact that it will not do an incomplete work. The cross of Roman times was a perfected killing instrument; it offered neither compromise nor concessions. If you stay on the cross, you can be sure that it will finish what has been started.

An old friend of mine once put it very simply. He confessed, "I want to die to myself, and I want to be crucified with Christ. But I know that as soon as I can I will want to compromise myself away from the cross. What I need is a Roman guard at the foot of my cross to ensure that I never come down." He is absolutely right. The cross does not have just a one-time impact on our lives. And remember, none of us can die to another person's cross—each of us has to surrender to our own. Then we live our lives from that perspective. Because each cross is personal, Jesus said that we must take up our cross *daily* to follow him (Luke 9:23). That is the secret to moving on in God. The Lord does not *expect perfection*, but he does *celebrate progress*.

As we take up our personal cross and follow Jesus, the freedom he earned for us on his cross comes into play. The cross of Christ becomes the one effective means of slaying our evil nature and freeing us from its power—it is no longer a symbol of defeat

---

2. Ravi Zacharias, *The Grand Weaver* (Grand Rapids: Zondervan, 2007), 122.

but of ultimate victory. That is why I find the subject of this book so exciting. It is the one truth I want to address. The cross of Jesus and the life it brings—"dying to live"—is for us today.

Our challenge is to surrender everything we have and are to him: our money, gifts, time, and ambitions. Then we enter into the exciting discovery of all that he wants us to become. There might be some surprises. I wanted to be a politician but ended up a preacher, and I can confidently say from experience that my will was wrong and his leading was right. We may dread the idea of not fulfilling our own desires; but if our will is surrendered and our life is in his hands, then our real potential is secure.

This is not to suggest that we will all turn out the same way. John D. is one of the many interesting characters in our local church. He is kind, gracious, godly, and intriguing. As an example, he requests the middle seat when flying on an airplane. When I asked John D. about this, he explained that it allows him to talk to two people about finding Jesus. Now how intimidating can some people be, especially to those of us who prefer the aisle seat for our own comfort and privacy? John D. is aware of the gifts that God has given him, and he is ready to exercise his will to see them used, even when he might not want to do so. Others couldn't do what John D. does. But when we surrender our will, Jesus takes who we are and makes us into who we can become.

When Jesus called his followers to take up their cross, he said, "If anyone would come after me . . . " (Matthew 16:24). That means he gives us a choice in calling us to the cross—and there our life becomes lost in his.

Keep Your Turban On

It was a cool winter day in North India. Three women, two of them Westerners, were on their way to a secret rendezvous. The instructions they had been given were simple: drive to a particular street corner in a busy part of the city—and wait.

A motorcycle driver arrived and indicated that the women should follow him. They tried to keep up as they drove behind him. Streets and intersections flashed by as they weaved a circuitous route through the city. Finally they arrived at a very ordinary house and met a man wearing a turban, "Pastor George," who shared his amazing story.

It all began when two of George's brothers met Jesus, even though they were part of a traditional Sikh family. They were converted and baptized in a local Christian church. Then came the crunch. The church leaders, who were not Sikhs, told them in no uncertain terms, "Now that you are Christians you must take off your turbans." This created great consternation, because their identity and culture were symbolized by this headwear. They would lose their sense of self! Furthermore, their ability to introduce others in their community to Jesus depended on remaining within their culture. If they removed their turbans, then the opportunity to communicate Christ to those they had known all their lives would be sacrificed.

Commitment to Christ means being prepared to lose everything. These two converted Sikhs were prepared to lose it all when they were baptized. Conversion to Christianity is viewed as a serious insult to Sikh beliefs. Leaving their culture behind would be the easy choice—though separated from their background, they would enjoy a fairly comfortable life. Retaining their turbans in order to serve Jesus in such a hostile environment, on the other hand, could introduce them to a "living death"—where self-sacrifice, persecution, and even martyrdom were likely outcomes.

During this same time, George was in Japan, where a young Japanese woman joyfully shared with him her newfound faith in Jesus. She was not inhibited in the slightest to witness to a Sikh about life in Christ. George met Jesus through her testimony. Returning home, George, along with his two brothers, continued to grow in their faith. Soon six of the seven brothers in the family had come to faith in Jesus. Then their mother became gravely ill, and they were told she had only hours left to live. The newly converted Sikh family desperately prayed. She was healed, and she gloriously surrendered her life to Jesus Christ!

The news spread throughout their community, and soon people began coming to ask questions and find out more. But almost all of them came at night. They weren't prepared to reveal their fascination in the Christian God who healed people.

These nocturnal visits had incredible results. Pastor George and his brothers had little opportunity for sleep. So many people were responding that they had to convert the whole middle floor of their house into a meeting place. As a group, Sikhs have always been closed to the gospel of Jesus Christ. Nevertheless, in one year Pastor George baptized two hundred people, with nearly all of them making their spiritual home in that small space. Drawn initially by the healing miracles that were regularly taking place, and then convicted by the truth of Jesus, they found saving faith in Christ. They joined a spiritual family who had sold out to Jesus Christ and became part of a people who had surrendered their will to his.

The three women discovered that the great lengths they went to in order to hear this story of crucified life were worth it. They share a valuable lesson from Pastor George: a life given over to the will of God may well involve keeping your turban on!

Going the Whole Way

That kind of faith is infectious. The story of a dangerous commitment, a hostile environment, clandestine motorcycle journeys, and secret nocturnal visits pulls us in with its excitement. Yet secret rendezvous and meetings at night are nothing new. Two thousand years ago one of the leading Jewish spiritual teachers, Nicodemus, initiated a nocturnal meeting with Jesus (John 3:1–2). In doing so, he risked his reputation, position, security, and destiny. He laid everything on the line—always the best place to start.

This meeting gave Jesus the opportunity to explain to Nicodemus that regardless of his age he needed to be "born again." The idea of being transplanted into his mother's womb was laughable, but eventually Nicodemus got the message. What Jesus wanted was for Nicodemus to give up—to relinquish his trust in past achievements and to abandon all faith based on his own understanding, past experiences, and present prestige. Instead, he was to start again—not from a position of power, but from one of powerlessness.

Fortunately this Jewish leader came to Jesus at his moment of greatest need. He was looking for the truth. There were others who also turned to Jesus as a last resort.

- When Jairus, a synagogue ruler, knew beyond a doubt that his daughter was dying, he came to Jesus (Mark 5:21–23).
- When her financial resources were completely exhausted and doctors were unable to help, a woman who had been hemorrhaging for twelve years touched Jesus without asking permission—because he was her last resort (Mark 5:24–28).
- When a man who had been an invalid for thirty-eight years was unable to enter the pool of Bethesda first when the water was stirred, Jesus went to him and told him to get up and walk. And the man did get up and walk, because he was instantly cured (John 5:1–9)!
- When a large crowd sat hungry and in need of food after listening to Jesus, they discovered, along with the disciples, that five loaves of bread and two fish were more than enough (Mark 6:34–44).

Little has changed today. Jesus still comes to us, even if we are not aware of our need for him. It began when he stood on the shore of Lake Galilee and challenged a group of ordinary fishermen to "Follow me" (Matthew 4:18–22).

Three things about this situation strike me as unusual. First, Jesus offered these first disciples a change of vocation: now they would catch people to be liberated rather than fish to be sold. Second, they left behind their possessions (boats and nets) as well as their families. Third, they responded decisively and completely when they were called.

These men had certainly not run out of options, but now they would discover a whole new dimension to life. In leaving their boats, they would find their life calling. They were likely in their teens or early twenties. Most of life still lay ahead, and yet they risked everything on this new teacher. Andrew told his brother Peter, "We have found the Messiah" (John 1:41). They followed him, leaving their comfort zones behind them.

The situation is similar to that of Pastor George and his brothers. Jesus wants to bring us out of our comfort zones and introduce us to a new security—that of his transforming love and power. Jesus may not always offer happiness based on external circumstances, but he does bring us deep significance and lasting inner joy. His method will vary, but it will match our ability to cope. The call to discipleship will be instant for some and more progressive for others, because Christ tenderly knows our differences.

When the rich young ruler was challenged to abandon his material possessions to follow Jesus, he couldn't leave them behind (Mark 10:17–22). It seemed that Jesus expected too much of him, and he went away an unhappy man. A life of true discipleship to Jesus carried too expensive a price tag. Was it really necessary for this man to give away all he owned in order to receive the life Jesus offered? If we were in Jesus' shoes, we might have run after the young man and offered a compromise or at least settled for a tithe of 10 percent. Jesus didn't let people off lightly. He demanded surrender to a life of discipleship that would cost everything.

Pastor George and most of the Sikhs he has baptized know this kind of surrender. Would we be as prepared to give this level of commitment?

Walking with Jesus

More than seven hundred years before the birth of Jesus Christ, God spoke to one of his prophets, a shepherd named Amos. This man had asked a significant question that predicted our walk of discipleship. He inquired, "Do two walk together unless they have agreed to do so?" (Amos 3:3). His rhetorical question anticipates no for an answer. The call to discipleship is a call to *partner with a person!* This is what any Jewish religious leader—even the openhearted Nicodemus—might struggle to understand. It was not primarily about obedience to the Ten Commandments or to the 613 related rules and regulations identified by the Jewish religious leaders. The heart of the Christian faith lies not in what you do, but in who you know. This is the prime distinctive of Christianity. It is not a *religion about God*; it is a *relationship with God.*

Amazingly, it is the Son of God who invites us on our journey with him. His journey led to a cross, and so may ours; but we know it will not end there. Christ in us represents the certainty of eternal glory (Colossians 1:27). He offers to take us into the intimacy of a relationship that his early disciples knew: loving him, serving him, talking with him, and learning from him. This is still the way Jesus makes disciples. As we spend time with him—in prayer, in his Word, and with other disciples in the community—and obey what he calls us to do, our nature begins to change. We begin to internalize the worldview that Jesus introduced. As Peter Maiden so crisply summarizes, "The call to discipleship is the call to relationship."[3]

There is a price tag attached. Walking with Jesus will require that we "throw off everything that hinders and the sin that so easily entangles" (Hebrews 12:1). Our Lord has things to do through us and places for us to go with him. We can't be weighed down if we want to keep up.

Choosing to Die

We were created to live in relationship with God. But human sin separated us from him. The call to discipleship is a call to recover our relationship and rediscover all that the living God intended us to be. Who could be better to learn from than Jesus himself? As the Argentinean church leader Juan Carlos Ortiz explains, "Discipleship is more than getting to know what the teacher knows. It is getting to be what he is."[4] The disciples learned what it meant to be like Jesus by spending time with him and practicing what he did.

This is where the cost of ongoing discipleship kicks in. The most casual reading of any of the Gospels shows how different Jesus was from the Jewish, Roman, Greek, and pagan cultures of the day. He turned the assumptions, priorities, motivations,

3. Peter Maiden, *Discipleship* (Colorado Springs: Authentic, 2007), 15.
4. Juan Carlos Ortiz, *Disciple: A Handbook for New Believers* (Orlando, FL: Strang Communications, 1995), quoted in Maiden, *Discipleship*, 22.

and commitments of the religious leaders of his day completely upside down. Then he called his disciples to do the same.

Many Christian leaders devise a "must do" list for their followers. Today it might include:

- Pray at least half an hour a day.
- Attend church twice a week.
- Tell one person a day about Jesus.
- Read the Bible through each year.

Although these are helpful disciplines, they can also become burdensome, lifeless routines. And besides that, Jesus had higher standards! He never taught his followers to neglect helpful disciplines; he just wanted them to go beyond them. So he taught the hallmarks of discipleship, instructing his follwers to:

- Love and pray for their enemies, not just for friends (Matthew 5:43–48).
- Leave everything behind to follow Jesus (Luke 14:25–33).
- Hold to the teachings of Jesus and faithfully pass them on (John 8:31–32).
- Consistently give their life for his glory, and bear much fruit as living evidence that he is at work (Matthew 16:24; John 15:8).

This rabbi, Jesus, was clearly countercultural—both then and now. He challenged people to become all they could be. He instructed his disciples that, after he was gone, they should go and make "Christians." . . . Well, not exactly.

They should make "converts." . . . No, that's not what he said.

"Go and make *disciples*" (Matthew 28:19). . . . Got it!

Jesus was seeking the development of people who were sold out to him, those who would leave their modern-day nets to follow him. That is the character of a true disciple, and that is the nature of one who will finish the race well.

Another metaphor for following Jesus is the Hollywood adaptation of the story of the Roman slave Spartacus.[5] Spartacus led a rebellion of slaves against Rome, an insurrection that proved to be surprisingly successful. But finally the rebel army was defeated, and many of the soldiers, including Spartacus, were captured. The reprisal dictated against him was that he be crucified. But initially none of the Roman officers were able to identify Spartacus. So they demanded that he step forward. One by one his followers did so, declaring "I am Spartacus." The road to Rome was lined with the crosses of those determined to die with their leader.

Spartacus may be a fictionalized account, but being prepared to live and to die for Jesus is no mere abstract concept. His call upon our lives is to experience every day what it means to be sold out, offering ourselves to him, for that is the nature of a true disciple.

---

5. Stanley Kubrick, *Spartacus*, (Universal Pictures, 1960)

Prayer ▶ Dear Lord, I open to you my hidden assumptions about my life and future. I give my dreams to you. Lead me into the deeper joy of your presence, and let my heart see others who need you as you see them. I don't want to waste my life, looking back to say, "I have been blind." Teach me to truly give myself to you. Help me to love your Word and spend time with you. Teach me to walk with you every day. Please help me always to live as your true disciple. Amen.

Sacrifice

DIE FIRST!

In 1998 I was in Tegucigalpa, Honduras, to help in the aftermath of Hurricane Mitch, one of the deadliest hurricanes on record. The night before I was to help, I looked out from my hotel at the lights of Tegucigalpa to survey the damage. The image imprinted in my mind was swaths of blackness interspersed by little patches of flickering lights. Morning confirmed the picture. Three houses were standing beside seven that were destroyed. One road and its dwellings were intact; the next two were gone. The odor of dead bodies (estimated at ten thousand) was vivid testimony to the awful loss suffered by the little nation.

Walking through the desolation I came upon one house that remained standing. The crippled man who lived there was still lying on his ramshackle bed. Six feet of mud covered his dead body.

On another street a man surveyed the debris that had once been his home. "What are you looking for?" I asked. "My wife and my three children," he replied.

As I walked, surrounded by traumatized people wandering aimlessly, my eyes were drawn to a woman and her daughter who were striding purposefully. She told me they were going to church, and her look indicated that she believed everyone else should do the same.

Her house had been demolished. The market stall and produce by which she earned her living were all gone. Her possessions were buried. All she had left was her daughter and the clothes they wore.

I said the first thing that crossed my mind. "After all this, how can you just go off to church?" I immediately knew that I had misspoken. I had wanted to ask, "How has your faith survived this awful tragedy? And how can we help you?"

With an intense look she said, "I've lost my home, my possessions, and my business. But I still have Jesus. And in the end, he is all that I need." I was totally embarrassed. I realized that this was the kind of crucified life that spoke of spiritual greatness. At first glance this was just an ordinary woman on the streets of Tegucigalpa, but one short conversation revealed her to be a devoted disciple of Jesus.

Taking Risks for Christ

Are the faith and character belonging to this woman supposed to be "normal" in a Christian life? That is a good question, especially when her experiences may be far removed from what many Christians encounter. Too often our loving dependence upon God hangs on the sense that things are going well for us. The opposite experience can raise doubts and questions that might not otherwise enter our minds. Do we love God only in the good times?

On several occasions in Scripture Abraham is called the "friend" of God (2 Chronicles 20:7; Isaiah 41:8; James 2:23). Consider Abraham's life. In obedience to God's call, he moved out of his comfort zone in Ur of the Chaldeans to go to Canaan (Acts 7:2–5). Later he faced the ultimate test when God asked him to sacrifice his son Isaac (Hebrews 11:17–19). Abraham accepted the risk, ready to give up his son—the "only son" of God's promise and the object of his love and affection (Genesis 22:2). This was pure faith in action. And we are called to live the same way.

Paul challenges us to live a different life from those around us, to "offer [our] bodies as living sacrifices" (Romans 12:1). He undoubtedly had in mind people whose lives he had observed. Take, for example, a member of Paul's apostolic team to whom he pays tribute in his letter to the Philippian church. Epaphroditus was a humble, selfless, and compassionate servant of Jesus Christ. Because he lived to serve, he had little regard for his personal safety. Paul insisted that Epaphroditus be respected since his service had brought him close to death's door. "Welcome him in the Lord with great joy, and honor men like him, because he almost died for the work of Christ, risking his life to make up for the help you could not give me" (Philippians 2:30).

Paul uses a Greek word here that appears nowhere else in the New Testament: *paraboleuomai*, which means "to risk." Paul indicates that Epaphroditus risked his life. That meaning, however, is the light version; the word also has deeper meanings. Its best English translation is "to hazard" or "to gamble." This verb means "to play the gambler"; and that is exactly what Epaphroditus had been doing, not for his own benefit, but for that of his Christian brothers and sisters.

Nero—the violent, and probably insane, Roman emperor— had Christians dipped in pitch, placed in massive candleholders, and set aflame to illuminate the beauty of his gardens. As persecution spread, thousands faced the assault of wild animals in Roman arenas, and others were crucified as Jesus had been. Epaphroditus was only one of hundreds of early heroes of the Christian faith, most of whose names we do not know.

The same Greek word that Paul employed in regard to Epaphroditus later described a group of Christians who willingly and selflessly exposed themselves to danger in the cause of Christ. These risk-takers were nicknamed the *Parabolani*. Wanting to live out the gospel by physically embodying the message of Christ, they gave their lives voluntarily and never to gain their own advantage. They offered themselves solely for the benefit of others. When they learned of people who were sick, even afflicted with dangerous diseases, they risked everything to provide help. Dangerous criminals in primitive dungeons became the unlikely beneficiaries of care offered by the Parabolani—God's gamblers!

The Parabolani are first recorded living in the third century, in the great Roman city of Carthage in North Africa. At this time, the population of Carthage had been decimated by one of two great plagues occurring in the first five centuries of the church's existence. The impact of this plague was so massive that bodies lay abandoned on the streets—no one would accept responsibility for their burial. With bodies decaying in the African sun, the plague grew at an astonishing rate. So in AD 252, Cyprian, bishop of Carthage, took a band of young men and women, the Parabolani, to bury the dead bodies in the city. Not content with burying the dead, they also cared for the sick, jeopardizing their lives as they did so. Many lives were saved, but the Parabolani sacrificed their lives in order to model the love of Jesus for the citizens of Carthage.[1] Their extravagant love in action spoke louder than words ever could.

These early heroes of the faith knew that the crucified life was of paramount importance. They *literally* believed, along with the apostle Paul, that "to live is Christ and to die is gain" (Philippians 1:21). Their choices revolutionized the attitude of many people in Carthage toward the church as they demonstrated to their neighbors the impact Jesus Christ could make upon a life.

Today the Parabolani have largely been forgotten. Perhaps this is because Epaphroditus' gambling approach to Christianity has long been out of fashion. The lack of information about the Parabolani may have more to do with our reluctance to feel

---

1. William Barclay, *The Letters to the Philippians, Colossians, and Thessalonians* (Philadelphia: Westminster Press, 1975), 50.

uncomfortable. Nowadays we are far more confident speaking of the benefits of coming to Jesus rather than the price we may be called to pay to join our life with the living God. We entice people with the "offer" of all that life in Christ will bring. We speak of love, joy, peace, satisfaction, and fulfillment that come through loving him. This is all true, but some yearn that the spirit of the Parabolani might return among the people of God to demonstrate that we live for more than ourselves.

We would be foolish to deny all the gifts and blessings that God provides. But there is a catch: we are not blessed just to enhance ourselves; we are blessed so that God might make us a blessing to other people. As the Lord promised Abraham, "I will make you into a great nation and I will bless you; I will make your name great, and *you will be a blessing*" (Genesis 12:2; italics added). It is for this reason we are called to lay our lives on the line. We offer Christ to a hungry world by living as sacrifices for him. It is as if our lives had already been laid upon the altar of sacrifice—not to die, but to live for Jesus so that he can bless others through us.

Being a "Living Sacrifice"

God offers us life, but his offer makes claims on how we are to live. The word *if* in Scripture is often followed by the word *then*. As David prepared his son Solomon to be king, he reminded Solomon of the promise God had made before Solomon was even born: "If your descendants watch how they live, and if they walk faithfully before me with all their heart and soul, you will never fail to have a man on the throne of Israel"

(1 Kings 2:4). Tragically, the unfaithfulness of Solomon and his descendants caused their disqualification from the blessings God would have provided.

At its most basic level, Jesus' paradoxical message was this: *Those who give up their life for my sake will certainly find it. But those who try to save their life—those who hang on to their life and refuse to risk it for me—will lose it.* David instructed Solomon to give up his life for God's sake when he said, "Be strong, show yourself a man, and observe what the LORD your God requires: Walk in his ways, and keep his decrees and commands . . . so that you may prosper in all you do and wherever you go" (1 Kings 2:2–3). These verses communicate both a claim on the way Solomon was to live and the benefit of living such a life.

Death to our own desires is always the first step toward ongoing life in Christ. Jesus taught this through baptism, which symbolizes both death and rebirth (Matthew 3:13–17). And Paul wrote about the importance of baptism to our new life in Christ when he said, "We were therefore buried with him through baptism into death in order that, just as Christ was raised from the dead through the glory of the Father, we too may live a new life" (Romans 6:4). You may think the Christian faith would be easier if we focused only on living and completely avoided the idea of death. But we need to allow God to change our view of death.

Pieter Ernst, a medical doctor from South Africa, has allowed God to change his view of death, and he has lived a very different life because of it. Delaying a needed kidney transplant for himself, he trained and developed hundreds of indigenous mothers to serve as health workers in the neighboring country of Mozambique. Thousands of mothers and their babies regained health as a result. Out in the bush, which has become home to one of the fastest growing national churches in the world, visiting American pastors listened in amazement to the testimony of witch doctors converted as a result of observing this health work. Only after this was Dr. Pieter ready for his kidney transplant.

The story doesn't end there, however. I was serving as president of World Relief at the time and was returning home to the U.S. after visiting the Kosovar refugee camps in Albania. I had stopped off in the U.K. to preach the Sunday services at a good friend's church. After the last service, my friend broke the news to me: the Limpopo River in Africa had burst its banks. Hundreds of people had died, half a million were homeless, and many members of my staff were missing. Included among them was Dr. Pieter Ernst.

I immediately changed my itinerary and flew to Mozambique, where I joined those who were using small boats to rescue hundreds of people who had survived the flood by climbing trees. It was quite a sight to see snakes, rats, and people cohabiting on the same branches.

Dr. Pieter was still missing. Finally, four days later, he turned up unshaven and still wearing his pajama trousers. He explained how he had awakened during the night when the flood hit and rushed into a boat. After rescuing as many people as he could, he returned to the World Relief office. There he discovered that the office had been looted when the water began to subside. The money that had been carefully saved for his kidney transplant was gone. Without saying a word, he went back to his boat to help rescue more of the people he loved. In such people, the spirit of the Parabolani still lives.

Serving Him All Our Days

Much of the current teaching in the church concentrates on how to live for Jesus. It's time we gained a greater urgency to learn what it means to die with him. In Psalm 73, the psalmist confidently declares, "You guide me with your counsel, and afterward you will take me into glory" (Psalm 73:24). And the apostle Paul dismisses of our present sufferings compared with the eternal glory that is being prepared for us (Romans 8:18; 2 Corinthians 4:17; 2 Timothy 2:10). He knew that his present "dying" was nothing compared to the future "living" that lay ahead. He focused on "dying to live."

We see this idea throughout Scripture. The prophet Isaiah announced, "He will swallow up death forever. The Sovereign LORD will wipe away the tears from all faces; he will remove the disgrace of his people from all the earth. The LORD has spoken" (Isaiah 25:8). Hosea says, "I will ransom them from the power of the grave; I will redeem them from death" (Hosea 13:14). Paul wrote, "When the perishable has been clothed with the imperishable, and the mortal with immortality, then the saying that is written will come true: 'Death has been swallowed up in victory'" (1 Corinthians 15:54). The true symbols of Christianity are an empty cross, because Jesus completed all things necessary for our salvation, and an empty tomb, because Jesus defeated death.

A Christian dies *with* Christ and dies *in* Christ, sharing in the victory that our Lord Jesus has already achieved. "[Grace] has now been revealed through the appearing of our Savior, Christ Jesus, who has destroyed death and has brought life and immortality to light through the gospel" (2 Timothy 1:10). This work is not our responsibility. We cannot defeat death—only Jesus could do that—but we can now join our sacrifice with his and find that in dying we live. Out of death to ourselves we begin to experience resurrected life with Jesus.

In the words of General William Booth, founder of the Salvation Army, we are destined to be "promoted to glory." In line with the mission of the Parabolani, Booth called his followers "troops of blood and fire" and militantly challenged them to a life of utter abandonment to God and total discipleship to his Son.

Through the centuries more Parabolani emerge, often unheralded and unexpected. Ordinary people do extraordinary things to serve the one whose death demonstrated what he legitimately expected to receive from his followers. The Parabolani are not extinct! Although no longer an isolated brotherhood of the crucified life, they continue in every Christian who lives as though already dead.

Father Damien was a fit and healthy man when he entered the leper colonies of the Hawaiian Islands in 1865. Few paid attention to him until the day he spilled boiling water on himself and failed to notice the pain, signaling that he had contracted their dreaded disease. Dwelling among the lepers as one of them, he lived his life to glorify the kingdom of God. People recognized that one of the Parabolani, sent from God to draw near and live with them, had arrived.

Paul affirmed, "I have been crucified with Christ and I no longer live, but Christ lives in me" (Galatians 2:20). Jesus died for us, and we are bought with a price; so our lives should be dedicated to his use for whatever purpose he requires. This totally shifts our focus. We no longer live for ourselves, but rather we exist solely to obey the instructions of our Lord and King. As Paul reminded his young disciple, Timothy, "Endure hardship with us like a good soldier of Christ Jesus. No one serving as a soldier gets involved in civilian affairs—he wants to please his commanding officer" (2 Timothy 2:3–4).

The New Testament tells of many people who knew their lives needed to be laid on the line for the living God. Stephen was stoned to death as the first martyr, John the Baptist was beheaded, Peter was imprisoned, and Paul was shipwrecked. None of them died to ambitions or desires to gain favor with God. They just knew that their lives on earth would be brief and that their "citizenship" was in heaven, giving them a different set of priorities (Philippians 3:20).

Throughout history, Christians have followed this example. These individuals have inherited the legacy. They started out serving Jesus very much like you and me, but they became spiritual heroes. They rock the boat—they are the Parabolani! We need to follow in their footsteps.

Consider Jim Elliot, a young American who had a real impact on me when I was a child. He wrote in his diary, "He is no fool who gives what he cannot keep to gain that which he cannot lose." In 1956 Auca Indians in Ecuador speared Elliot and his four friends to death as they tried to bring them the love of Jesus.

Another such man, C. T. Studd, was captain of England's cricket team. Although he had great personal wealth and fame, he gave it all away. Sacrificing everything, he responded when God called him to serve as a missionary to China in 1885. In the midst of a difficult life of suffering and service, he wrote what amounted to a Parabolani obituary: "Let us see to it that the devil will hold a thanksgiving service in hell, when he gets the news of our departure from the field of battle."

Prayer ▶ Lord, I tremble to know what you have in store for my life. Whatever it is, I want to commit all I have and am into the arms of your love. Show me daily where you would have me serve you. Please supply the courage, boldness, sensitivity, and wisdom that I need to be a living sacrifice—for your glory! Amen.

CHAPTER SIX

Giving

THE ™ME SYNDROME

I was meeting with a well-known pastor. Not just any pastor, but a pastor among pastors. He was the author of numerous books, an established voice on radio broadcasts, and considered by many to be a legend in his time.

My task was to plead on behalf of churches in a distant country that needed some financial help. Their own people had raised 90 percent of the funds for a crucial and strategic project, but raising the last 10 percent had proven more difficult. The need was great, and the people had made huge personal sacrifices. Now if only their brothers and sisters would stand with them, they would be able to complete the project.

After I explained the situation, it was difficult to contain my emotions when this pastor replied, "Well, what's in it for us?"

I could hardly believe it. A national church had asked for help from those who had overflowing resources and who, frankly, could not use all of what they gathered. In the end, this pastor's church gave a very nominal contribution, and other churches responded in a similar way. The churches of the nation making the request were disappointed and struggled to try to bridge the financial gap.

I could not forget those words: "What's in it for us?" Why should there be anything? Can we not love and care for each other as the family of God?

Living in a "Me" Culture

Our culture encourages us to think there's no one higher to answer to, or to please, than ourselves. As a result, many people seem to live with the attitude that "It's all about me." We expect to get what we deserve, to receive our rights, to improve our living situation, and to climb the ladder of success.

Sometimes the "me" culture is just as alive in the church as it is in the general culture. Recently an elder of our church told me that he heard a mature Christian in our congregation remark, "I love Clive's preaching—it's so challenging. But he never makes me feel good about myself." Others report that some folks have left the church because they believe it is no longer focused on them and their needs. They are frustrated because there is too much emphasis on others in the community rather than on themselves. These might be legitimate objections. We must be ready to meet each other's needs and humble enough to recognize there are always lessons to be learned. However, at its core, the church is not essentially about *me*, but about *us* and how we relate to those around us. As we are reminded in Scripture, "Nobody should seek his own good, but the good of others" (1 Corinthians 10:24).

The concentration on *me* demands that the church meet my needs rather than encourage me to offer my life in obedience to Christ to serve the needs of others (Philippians 2:4). The church's mandate to be culturally relevant can become a dangerous snare. The challenge to meet the needs of new generations can become so distorted that we absorb the very cultural ideals we were trying to transform. The church that intended to change the world may discover that the world has succeeded in changing the church.

Reasons to Be Different

On the cross Jesus gave the supreme example of crucified love. Despite wrestling with indecision in the garden of Gethsemane, his conclusion was complete. "Not my will, but yours be done" (Luke 22:42). There was no compromise. That is the character of the crucified life.

Not content merely to *know* what is right, such a life must always *live out* that understanding. It was love that took Jesus to a cross. There was nothing in his life that deserved punishment. His compassion reached out to us, so it is not surprising that he expects compassion and sacrifice from his disciples today. When we fail to live up to his example, we discredit our Lord, and we can give the impression that Christians are no different from anyone else.

It was more than ten years ago when I first visited Rwanda. Like many of my generation, I was reared on stories about how East Africa was transformed by God in the mid-twentieth century. Now I could witness the results firsthand. But the first thing I noticed at the airport was the bullet holes. They were a vivid reminder that two years earlier Rwanda had experienced a horrible genocide. Hundreds of thousands of bodies still remained unidentified. The violence was officially over, yet fear and uncertainty still pervaded the atmosphere in the capital city of Kigali.

It was painful to recall that in the middle of the twentieth century Rwanda was known to the Western church for its spectacular role in the East African revival. This was one of the most exciting outbreaks of spiritual growth in modern history. As the years passed, the message continued, but the lifestyle was lost. Now the airport in Kigali tragically gave witness to a different truth. Tribal killing was alive and well, and the revival had died out.

At the time of my visit, I served as the president of World Relief, a Christian relief and development agency. On this trip I was particularly impressed by the quality of our Christian staff. One of those who stood out was Beatrice. Late one afternoon she broke into a flood of tears and shared a shocking story with my wife Ruth and I about the difficulty of serving Christ in post-genocide Rwanda.

The genocide in Rwanda had emerged from decades of tribal hatred between the Hutus and the Tutsis. Ethnically, our staff was pretty equally divided between the two, and there were a few instances of overt racial hatred. However, this was the post-genocide era, and memories of the awful atrocities that had taken place were still fresh. Beatrice's young husband was a pastor. They were highly talented people and deeply in love. The afternoon of our visit, a young man had visited the compound containing the World Relief offices. Many of the staff leaped up to greet him as a well-known brother in Christ. But the last time Beatrice had seen this man was during the genocide when he held her husband on the ground and viciously kicked him. Her husband could have died. Subsequently, there had been no restitution or apology.

Beatrice knew the staff from the other tribal group knew the story, yet they did not hesitate to enjoy a time of friendly fellowship with their Christian brother. To write off the beating Beatrice's husband received as an isolated incident would be wrong. After all, 900 thousand people died in an orgy of killing that raged across one of the most Christian places on the planet.

There were other people on the World Relief staff who acted as heroes during those days. Grasping the paradox of the crucified life, they understood that Christians should stand out from the crowd and live differently. Some risked their lives to save the lives of those who were regarded as their tribal enemies. They remembered the principles upon which the revival had been grounded, though others had forgotten the demands of the crucified life.

Jesus taught his disciples that they should have a radically different attitude toward their enemies than most would expect. "You have heard that it was said, 'Love your neighbor and hate your enemy.' But I tell you: Love your enemies and pray for those who persecute you" (Matthew 5:43–44). The apostle Paul underlined this in the instruction "If your enemy is hungry, feed him; if he is thirsty, give him something to drink" (Romans 12:20).

The tragedy is that so many of us are overwhelmed by the "me" syndrome. We have been brainwashed by our culture to such an extent that we cannot conceive of subordinating our self-interest for the benefit of others. That is an awful indictment upon our faith. Christ-followers are to be holy (the Greek word is *hagios*, which means "dedicated" or "consecrated"). This does not mean we separate from everyone else. It means that a life prepared to die with Christ is to be lived for others.

Living a New Life

True Christian faith begins with what I *lose*, not with what I *get*. Jesus said to his first disciples, "Whoever wants to save his life will lose it, but whoever loses his life for me will find it" (Matthew 16:25).

Too many of us have lived under a misconception. We thought that the presence of Jesus, the ministry of the church, and the Christian life were simply for us. There are those, including a myriad of TV evangelists, who claim that we are entitled to perfect health and all the wealth we could reasonably desire. Not so! How can this be the case since Jesus acknowledged, "Foxes have holes and birds of the air have nests, but the Son of Man has no place to lay his head" (Matthew 8:20)? Jesus and his disciples owned so little that when he and Simon Peter needed to pay their tax bill they had to borrow a coin from the mouth of a fish (Matthew 17:27). In every instance God provides—though to meet our basic needs, not to create a mountain of cash for our benefit.

The crucified life moves us from the "me" syndrome to the idea that the Christian life is not just about keeping me alive and well. Rather, it is about Christ living in me and through me (Galatians 2:20). Suddenly the emphasis moves from methods of self-improvement for my old life toward discovering a life in Christ that must be radically different. This is the heart of the issue. *Christianity is not a subculture that I acquire or an experience to add to my old way of living.*

Although the blessings of eternity do lie ahead of us, we are called in this life to serve Christ. In this gloriously upside-down kingdom, Jesus reverses all that we might expect or that the carnal Christian might want. It is not about me; it is about Jesus. Only in losing our lives to him can we find them again. As Jesus warned, "Any of you who does not give up everything he has cannot be my disciple" (Luke 14:33). His primary objective is not that we look to ourselves, but that we ask how God wants to equip us and make us the means by which he can bless others. Then we truly discover ourselves and our destiny.

At that point a real Christian is born—one who just might show the world the *something different* that has been desperately missing. As disciples of Christ, we will be doing the will of God from our heart (Ephesians 6:6), and that makes the hearts of others pay attention!

A few years ago a group of salesmen were running through Chicago's O'Hare Airport after a sales convention. They all had spouses and families expecting them home for Friday dinner, assuming that they reached their plane on time. In the rush to the gate one of them accidentally knocked over a vendor's table of apples. In spite of the apples rolling across the terminal floor, all but one of the men caught the plane in time.

This one person paid attention to the tug of compassion for the girl whose table had been knocked over. He told his buddies he'd be on the later flight, and none offered to join him. He walked back to the place where people were still dodging the scattered apples, and he was soon glad that he did.

The sixteen-year-old apple seller was blind. Down on her hands and knees, she was groping for the spilled produce, unable to assess how much each was damaged. So the salesman did it for her. He picked up the apples, examined them, and gave her forty dollars for the battered fruit. When the job was done, he apologized to the tearful and bewildered blind girl and turned to find a later flight. As he walked away, he heard the girl quietly ask, "Are you Jesus?" Taken aback, he paused mid-stride and thought, *Wasn't this well worth the delay?*

Let's face it. For most of us Christians the idea of being mistaken for Jesus is highly appealing. Deep down we long to so resemble Jesus that our world would struggle to tell the difference. Like me, perhaps you would want to be that salesman. I wish my life was so lost in God that I would have responded as he did. The trouble is that I know myself too well.

Under New Management

The fellow who went back to the apple seller responded in a wholly different way than the others. They responded with their "fleshly" desires; these are the impulses that once controlled our lives. Yet Scripture reminds us, "We know that our old self was crucified with him so that the body of sin might be done away with, that we should no longer be slaves to sin" (Romans 6:6). Here is the key. The fleshly impulse that rules our lives must be *condemned to death*. The only thing that Christ can do for the rule of the old self is to kill it. The instrument of death to the flesh is a cross.

It is hard to find many positive things to say about life on a cross. You cannot come down from it voluntarily. You cannot dismiss the disgrace of your position. You cannot determine your future from a cross. There is one positive thing to say. Life from a cross is the perfect antidote to the "me" syndrome. Viewed from the cross, *my* life, *my* rights, and *my* future no longer lie in my power or in my hands. In fact, my life can only follow his instructions, and my task is simply to obey his leading.

Jesus does not respond to our demands, but he does offer us all that he knows is necessary for our lives. He calls us to be open to his instruction. Rather than blessing our own agenda, he wants to undertake the direction for us. That is the reason God's great gift to Saul of Tarsus on the road to Damascus was to make him blind. When Paul could not see where he was going, he needed to ask for direction. Even after regaining his eyesight, Paul was content to rely on God's guidance. He could confidently announce, "For to me, to live is Christ and to die is gain" (Philippians 1:21). For Paul, the governance of "me" had finally and irretrievably broken down. He had discovered how to blindly follow his God.

And so must we.

Prayer ▶ Father, in a world where everything revolves around me, I long to be different. Help me to live selflessly for others. Please live in me so the world may see the reality of your love and life demonstrated in all I say and do. To the glory of your name, Amen.

CHAPTER SEVEN

Exchange

A ROYAL TRANSFER

Have you ever wanted to be different? Not just an improved version of yourself, but a whole different character in life? It is a common fantasy: to be born as a completely different person. Some would be a princess or a president; others would live as a business tycoon or a rock star. Whatever the fantasy, it begins with the desire to change something about yourself that you are unsatisfied with.

Here is a story from my youth that I've never told publicly. I have always loved sports—watching them rather than participating in them. I always wanted to play sports when I was young, but I was rarely selected because I wasn't very good! One day when I was fourteen, though, an opportunity arrived. My school was short a participant for the one-mile race. No one else was eligible because they were involved in other activities. It wouldn't matter where I placed, since only three other runners were registered for the event. All I had to do was to show up at the finish line. Even if I came in last, I would gain one point for the team!

After carefully thinking things through, I decided to run. But I didn't want to make a fool of myself in front of my friends and the visiting parents. So I trained hard to get ready for my big opportunity. My parents bought new running shoes for me, and I imagined myself running to win.

The final curve of the last lap remains in my mind to this day. Although I was behind the other three runners, the guy in front of me was not far ahead. If only I could come in third instead of last. Poised to move past him, I knew I was ready to meet the challenge . . . but I just couldn't do it. I finished the race, but I came in last. My brief athletic career ended.

So many of us live with an internal contradiction. We want to be different, but some ingredient is missing. So we try to be satisfied with less than the desire of our hearts.

Change Comes from God

God desires us to be different from the world around us, but real change must be based on his perspective rather than on ours. An example of this is Moses. After his childhood rescue from Pharaoh's extermination squads, he spent forty years in the palace—feeling, as a prince of Egypt, that he was "somebody." But when he spotted an Egyptian abusing a Hebrew, one of his own people, Moses murdered the Egyptian in retaliation. Since his action was seen by others, he fled for his life into the wilderness of Midian. He spent the next forty years herding sheep in desolate areas, realizing every day that he had become "nobody."

Alone with his flock one day on "the far side of the desert," Moses saw a bush that was on fire but not burning up (Exodus 3:1–2). Out of that bush, God called Moses to do more, and *be* more, than seemed possible to Moses. So reluctant Moses employed a mountain of excuses to explain to the Lord why this "nobody" could never be "somebody" again. But none of these excuses persuaded God. He knew something that Moses didn't. God knew that the issue wasn't changing Moses; instead, it was a matter of Moses learning that *God could live through him.*

Simon Peter learned the same lesson. He was the first to recognize and affirm who Jesus was: the Messiah and the Son of God (Matthew 16:16; John 6:69). Such statements were dangerous. They could have precipitated a charge of blasphemy, especially if heard by the Jewish religious leaders. Yet just weeks later Peter denied knowing Jesus. Not once, not twice, but three times he passionately disowned his friend and Lord. Desperate tears came as Peter realized his own courage and confidence hadn't been enough to overcome fear; he had done the very thing he had promised not to do (Mark 14:72).

If these great men of faith could not direct their own destiny or change their own lives, then what hope is there for us? How were their lives eventually transformed? Did they learn to work harder? Or does the revolution of one's life need to originate with God rather than with the individual?

Do-It-Yourself Christianity

Often we respond to our need to change by trying harder. We seek the advice of books, CDs, sermons, and articles that tell us how we can become different. The notion of trying harder can sound incredibly "Christian." But is it really? It began near the end of the nineteenth century with the Victorian author Samuel Smiles and his little book entitled *Self-Help*. This theme has been reworked through movements and methods from Moral Re-Armament to the ABCs of Conversion (Accept, Believe, Confess, Decide). Each offers a simple process: we take action, and we change our lives. Of course, such simple remedies often miss the point.

Rather than the clamor of "try harder," "do better," "give more," "go further," and "work at it," could God be asking for something different? Just as Moses tried to fulfill God's purpose by killing the Egyptian, our activities can be counterproductive. Even with the best motivation in the world, Moses became a murderer rather than a missionary.

Our world is full of people urging us toward self-improvement. Isn't it time to "be still" and "wait for God" instead of trying to do it all for him? Perhaps we are beyond improvement. Are we too far gone for subtle change to effect any major difference?

Scripture teaches that in our fleshly capacity we cannot genuinely be altered or really make a difference for God. The apostle Paul had to learn this lesson. He openly acknowledged, "I have the desire to do what is good, but I cannot carry it out. For what I do is not the good I want to do; no, the evil I do not want to do—this I keep on doing" (Romans 7:18–19). His conclusion was that in his sinful nature he could only be a slave to sin (Romans 7:25). Through his own efforts he could never fulfill God's intention for his life.

Yet, we long for a program that will finally bring us into all that God has prepared for us. But just when we think we have arrived, we discover that such a path is an illusion. It never takes us far enough. Still, we try to produce the change that only God can bring.

Does this mean that we need not discipline ourselves to spend time in God's Word? Does it mean letting our minds stray rather than focusing on the practice of prayer? Is it okay to shirk commitments to others because we don't hear God telling us to fulfill our obligations? No, of course not! Spiritual disciplines are good and necessary, but without the presence of God they are inadequate and lead us nowhere. The question is whether these efforts will deliver the amazing do-it-yourself transformation we long for; or do we need some other help to complete this inner renovation?

The final conclusion is that no study, discipline, self-assessment, spiritual experience, author, or program—even if helpful—has ever succeeded in making us the people in God we want to be. Face up to it: we somehow always fall short of achieving it for ourselves.

Try Exchanging Lives

It was Christmastime and I was speaking to several hundred young people at a carol service. The challenge I faced was to explain why a baby born in a manger two thousand years ago was relevant to their lives right there and then. I was in Europe, where there is a greater awareness of soccer than Scripture, so I tried a sporting analogy. I selected one young fellow and asked him to imagine playing football like one of the stars of the last fifty years. I told him to imagine the spirit of Pelé, Eusébio, or George Best invading his life and giving him the power to play like a star. How different would his life be?

Some years later that man told me the illustration caused him to start thinking about spiritual matters. He eventually exchanged his life, and today he is a preacher. That is why Jesus came, not just to be believed in or talked about, but so that we might surrender our lives to him and allow his life to be lived through us.

Could it be that some of us have been looking in the wrong direction or to the wrong source? When we begin to look up toward Jesus, rather than down toward ourselves, we begin to take hold of the right answer. The true secret of Christianity is not a *changed* life, but an *exchanged* life, as we stop trying to live for God and allow him to live through us.

When Peter realized that he could not remain faithful to Jesus, even with his good intentions, he wept (Mark 14:66–72). When Paul understood that Jesus really was the Lord, he was blinded and led by the hand to a home in Damascus (Acts 9:1–9). When Moses realized that an ordinary bush could be filled with God, he was commanded to take off his shoes, for he was standing on holy ground (Exodus 3:1–5).

Each experience was a deep response to the presence of God:

- To be so filled with remorse for past failures that you weep.
- To be so dependent for direction that you no longer know where you are going in your own strength.
- To humble yourself and stop trying to become "somebody," knowing that God can fill the most unlikely of people and bring transformation—for his glory.

Here we begin to see it is not our *abilities* that God is after. Nor is he just seeking the opportunity to *refine* those abilities. No, it is our *availability* and *dependency* that he wants so that he can do what he wills in us. Living a victorious Christian life does not begin with a program or a technique, but with an understanding. Paul demonstrates this when he states that the entire purpose of his life is to "gain Christ and be found in him" (Philippians 3:8–9). The essence of Christianity does not lie in me trying to live for Jesus, but in knowing the truth that "I no longer live, but Christ lives in me" (Galatians 2:20).

Looking Up

Here is a revolutionary principle: life doesn't depend upon me, but upon Jesus! "If we live, we live to the Lord; and if we die, we die to the Lord. So, whether we live or die, we belong to the Lord" (Romans 14:8). It is not about me, as I gaze down at all my weaknesses and failings. No, it is about him and my gaze upward to the one who longs to do it all in me. "For to me, to live is Christ and to die is gain" (Philippians 1:21).

Gazing up guarantees that we are looking in the right direction. Two laws, or principles, are at work:

- When I fix my eyes upon Jesus, then I take them off me.
- When I take my eyes off myself, then I can see Jesus.

Keith Green, the late singer and songwriter, observed, "It's so hard to see when my eyes are on me." We have been encouraged to examine ourselves, when we should be looking at Christ. The message of God's love is that he comes to reign *in* us. In other words, as we give our lives to him, he gives his life to us. It truly is a royal transfer, my life exchanged with the King. "For you died, and your life is now hidden with Christ in God. When Christ, who is your life, appears, then you also will appear with him in glory" (Colossians 3:3–4).

Now we can appreciate the difference. It's not about us having to live *for him*, but about allowing him full permission to invade our lives and live *through us*. That way it will be "God who works in you to will and to act according to his good purpose" (Philippians 2:13). This purpose may be way outside our own plans.

The future looked bright for Pastor Walcir and his family. This Brazilian pastor was being offered a pastorate in the United States. He and his wife, Ivonilce, and their three daughters could relocate, accept a much higher salary, and care for a Brazilian congregation in the heart of America.

What God chose for them, however, was different: a small congregation located up the Amazon River in a clearing adjacent to the jungle. The girls had to be placed in a school away from their mom and dad. But, oh how God blessed Pastor Walcir and Ivonilce! Their outreach was used to bring people to Jesus, the little church grew, and their daughters became fine young women of God.

Was it what they would have chosen? Probably not. But life "in Christ," by definition, is not designed by us. We take what he gives us. It is no longer about my words spoken for him, but about his words spoken through me. It is no longer about my attempt to serve him, but about his Spirit working through me. It is no longer about my efforts to change my life, but about his love transforming me. "Christ in you, the hope of glory" (Colossians 1:27). That is what Pastor Walcir discovered, and he and his wife are only two among millions.

Living with Power from Above

Even though Jesus is God's Son, he said that he could do nothing by himself, that he could do only what he saw his Father doing (John 5:19; 8:28). He lived in total dependence upon his Father, and that is how he wants us to relate to him.

Herein lies true liberty and independence. We are set free from our own resources and given the vast potential that comes when we live "in Christ" and he lives in us. In our world today, the Lord Jesus Christ comes to those who exchange their lives for his. This is exactly what he provided through his life on earth some two thousand years ago. He pointed to himself as the vine; his disciples were to be nothing more, or less, than branches. He said we could do nothing *apart from him*, which means we can do everything *through his life in us* (John 15:5).

We may wonder, "Where and when does this exchange take place?" The answer is that sometimes we first have to exhaust all "do-it-yourself" efforts and all other options. Only then are we finally prepared to give in. Most of the time, we would much prefer to do something for ourselves.

In the 1970s, I had hair halfway down my back and wore clothes that were in fashion at that time. I was at a clergy conference when an ex-army major arrived to address us. He arrived with military precision, wearing impeccably tailored clothing. Major Ian Thomas was horrified that a preacher of the gospel could show up looking the way I did. He did get over it, fortunately; and we grew to appreciate and respect each other.

I was greatly moved by Major Thomas' story. Having come to faith when he was fifteen, he longed to serve as a medical missionary in Nigeria. Consumed with the excitement of his new faith, he spent every moment seeking to reach people with the love of Christ. He even started a youth club in my old haunts amid the slums of London's East End. But one night as Ian reviewed the little he had achieved, his heart felt heavy with the conviction that, despite all this activity, he was a hopeless failure. God cracked open his heart. Through Ian's bitter tears, it was as if the Lord were saying, "Seven years with utmost sincerity you have been trying to live *for* Me, on My behalf, the life that I have been waiting for seven years to live *through* you."[1]

---

1. Ian Thomas, quoted by V. Raymond Edman, Introduction to *The Saving Life of Christ*, by W. Ian Thomas (Grand Rapids: Zondervan, 1988), 11 (italics in original).

When Major Thomas shared this part of his story, I was devastated. My heart was gripped with a similar feeling. We often reach this point when we have finally run out of rope; we have exhausted all our efforts to do God's work and realize that our best efforts produce little or no fruit. This is when we are ready to die to our self-effort and to live by God's grace within us. Why, that opens it all up! We finally recognize that only God himself can fill the God-shaped hole in our lives.

Major Thomas himself once wrote these words: "To be *in Christ*—that is redemption; but for Christ to be *in you*—that is sanctification! To be *in Christ*—that makes you fit for Heaven; but for Christ to be *in you*, that makes you fit for earth! To be *in Christ*—that changes your destination; but for Christ to be *in you*—that changes your destiny! The one makes Heaven your home—the other makes this world his workshop."[2]

Many of us would like the opportunity to live the life of Jesus. The key is first sharing in the death of Jesus. Here we confront the main difficulty. For most people, the price tag is way too high. We want to do all the living, and we want Jesus to do all the dying. What he really wants is for us to know the reality of dying so that he can come and do the living in our lives. Dying to live—the paradox of the crucified life.

The remarkable thing is that he changes not just what we do, but what we want to do. This is the unique job of his Spirit. And Paul urges believers: "Do not conform any longer to the pattern of this world, but be transformed by the renewing of your mind.

---

2. W. Ian Thomas, *The Saving Life of Christ* (Grand Rapids: Zondervan, 1961), 22 (italics in original).

Then you will be able to test and approve what God's will is—his good, pleasing and perfect world" (Romans 12:2). This is what it means to be a new creature in Christ. Many of us have learned the Lord Jesus requires a different level of discipleship. He does not expect that we try harder to work for him. Instead, he longs to live and work through us. That is the real exchange.

Although it may have questionable authenticity, a fitting story is told about Winston Churchill. With enormous pride, a young man said to the great prime minister, "I am a self-made man." Churchill replied, "Young man, you have just relieved God of an awesome responsibility." The miracle is that our God waits to do his work in us. We must never try to do his job for him.

Prayer ▶ Not my desires, but yours, Lord. Not my way, but yours, Lord. Not my abilities and strengths, but yours, Lord. Speak freely to me throughout each day. Tune my heart to yours. I freely consecrate my whole being to you. But I ask one thing: Would you exchange my life for yours? Thank you, Lord. In Jesus, Amen.

CHAPTER EIGHT

Dying

LIVING ON THE FAR SIDE OF THE CROSS

The silhouette of three crosses stood starkly against the sky. Two criminals hung on either side of Jesus. His hands and feet had been securely nailed to the wood, and he had been left to die. The pain was excruciating as he shifted his weight from his hands to his feet and then back again. One thing was obvious: despite the mocking suggestions from the crowd, no one was going to take him down. Asphyxiation lurked ahead, and then death would come (although in Jesus' case it didn't take as long for him to die as with typical asphyxiation, since he died—literally—from a broken heart).

There is no predicament less safe on earth than being nailed to a cross.

The earliest Christians were delightfully extreme. Many of them sold what they possessed and put their lives at risk to spread the message of Jesus. Some of them had seen the empty tomb with their own eyes. All of them had witnessed the power of changed lives. They knew their crucified Messiah was alive, and they had received his Holy Spirit.

A. W. Tozer depicted this with wonderful clarity: "The church began in power, moved in power and moved just as long as the Lord gave power. When she no longer had power, she dug in for safety and sought to conserve her gains."[1] These men and women were comfortable out on a limb; in the power of the Lord, they were turning their world upside down (Acts 17:6).

Doesn't it seem strange that so many Christians cling to safety when risky living should be the order of the day? Why are many of us more easily identified with respectability than with healthy extremism? The phrase "What would Jesus do?" is often used to caution against improper behavior rather than to encourage living on the edge, as Jesus did. While Jesus' criticisms posed a threat to respectable religious people, he welcomed those who were struggling, imperfect, and nonreligious.

Jesus drank from the cup of a Samaritan woman, dined with tax collectors, and touched the lepers, the blind, and the bleeding. He spent his time with the people whom "religious" people despised. What ultimately landed Jesus on a cross may have been his radical commitment to the idea that ordinary, but broken, people could become world-transforming men and women of God. What madness. What glory!

---

1. A. W. Tozer, *Paths to Power* (London: Oliphants, 1964), page number unknown.

Jesus' critics thought he rocked the boat at a time when relations with Rome were unstable. He ate with the wrong people and visited the wrong places, while respect for religious leadership was being questioned by Jewish people and by the Roman state. He opened the doors of his kingdom to people of any ethnic or religious background—just when the Jews were trying to recapture their religious exclusivity.

Instead of making things better, Jesus appeared to make things worse. He could make nomads out of those who would otherwise be settled citizens and enemies out of those who would otherwise be friends. His emphasis on discipleship created tension and disruption in families. He pointed people to rebel against their spiritual leaders rather than against the occupying forces of Rome. He claimed to be the only Son of God while under the state rule of an emperor who claimed to be the son of a god. Jesus was introducing a new kingdom, one in which God reigns!

Jesus' passion for changed lives reaches out to *all* people, calling any who will receive his love and surrender to him. When we turn in repentance to God, we enter into what may well be a turbulent journey. He offers a roller-coaster ride rather than a soft and sedentary passage through life. All around the world, the people of God are waking up to the message that serving Christ is no soft or easy option. This thread runs throughout Paul's writings to the early church. It is dangerous to live for Christ here on earth. The safety of heaven comes later!

A Great Challenge

It was Christmas Eve in London. For twelve years we had lived in our three-story Victorian house, happily bringing up our family in this inner-city home. The house was festooned with Christmas decorations, presents were still being surreptitiously wrapped in different bedrooms, and everyone was busily preparing for the big day.

I don't remember where I had gone. Perhaps I went out with one of the children to make a last-minute purchase. Or maybe I just went for a walk with the dog (a liver-spotted Dalmatian named Tozer). But when I walked in the door I saw that my wife, Ruth, was as white as a sheet. It was almost as if she had seen a ghost.

Gradually the story unfolded. A telephone call from America had come straight out of the blue. Ruth and I had been invited to go for an interview in the States, with the possibility of becoming the next president of World Relief, a sixty-year-old international, church-based relief and development agency. The look on Ruth's face told me everything. This was something she thought could well become a reality. And it did.

For many this would sound like the opportunity of a lifetime. For us, it was a Calvary we had to face. Please don't misunderstand me. If you have to leave your relatives, friends, and homeland behind in order to relocate halfway around the world, then the United States can be a wonderful place to be invited to live. The fact that we are still in America well over ten years later says a lot.

At the time, however, things seemed very different. We have four children. Our two daughters were not a problem. Vicky was leaving a university and heading off to serve the Lord overseas; and Suzy, at thirteen, was young enough for her education to be interrupted by moving to the United States.

Now the boys—they were another story. Both were at a point in their education that could not be disrupted. If we left for the States, they would have to stay behind. But then, when their education would allow them to leave the U.K., they would be too old for family immigration. Facing a permanent family division into separate continents was bad enough, but soon our cross took on larger proportions. Gavin was our happy-go-lucky seventeen-year-old. His verdict was simple. "How can a God of love break up a family like ours?" His older brother, Kris, was more blunt. "If that is the kind of God that we love and serve, then he can shove it!"

We prayed, tested our decision, received counsel from friends . . . and ultimately we reluctantly obeyed the call God placed upon our lives. Both Ruth and I knew the bitter truth: our two much-loved lads would leave the church and Jesus the day we left the U.K.

The next months were awful. We will always be grateful to those who tried to understand and share a little of our pain. Ruth wept a lake of tears; and, frankly, I wondered if the Lord really did know what he was doing. If this was to be my cross, then I couldn't wait to get to the other side.

Beyond the Cross

Each of us is saddened by the cross when we sense what Jesus must have suffered for us. At the same time, we recognize that his death brings light to our darkness and life to our death. By way of the cross, God offers us the miracle of divine forgiveness and a divine new beginning in all its fullness. Through Christ's death on the cross, we receive life that cannot be vanquished or defeated, life like no other, and life that brings his power. All of this, however, can come only via a cross.

The tragic reality is that we are "damaged goods." But we can be restored through divine power. It is only when we admit that we cannot change ourselves that he provides his supernatural transformation. It is only when we confess our failure to live the way he intended that he comes to change our hearts and lives. This change begins at the cross. Divine change requires that we first commit to trust God, whom we are coming to know and love. This trust demands faith. Faith results in action, action requires obedience, and obedience comes from our dependence on him.

This all sounds great in theory. But it can come across differently when we are enduring a crash course in practice. The living God sets before us two options: either we function apart from the cross, living by our own energies and abilities but unable to move forward, or we live on the other side of the cross. Here we live regenerated by Christ and aware of God's voice, power, and transforming love. We then live from his resources—moving forward and *not* looking back.

Again, this may sound fine. But the primal scream still remains: "It is not supposed to cost me my family!"

Moses addressed this issue with the people of Israel in vivid and unforgettable words: "This day I call heaven and earth as witnesses against you that I have set before you life and death, blessings and curses. Now choose life, so that you and your children may live and that you may love the LORD your God, listen to his voice, and hold fast to him. For the LORD is your life" (Deuteronomy 30:19–20). There you have it in a nutshell. The children are involved too. That is what my wife and I discovered for ourselves.

Nine months after we moved I preached at a festival in the U.K. At the back of the large tent, which held several thousand people, were the boys. Their paths back to Jesus were as different as their personalities, but they both made it back. Today all four of our children serve Jesus in very different ministries. We enjoy a unity forged via the cross. Gavin says, "I was living off your faith; I just needed the space to discover my own." The memories often come flooding back, bringing tears to my eyes, when I listen to him preach. Sometimes Gavin will say, "I never knew what it really meant to love Jesus until my dad left me for him." That's how I know that he understands.

Dreams and ambitions, friends, and yes, even families have to be surrendered at the cross, but only when Father God requires them in order to work out his purposes. For then life will be radiantly different; it will be transformed on the far side of the cross.

Beginning Again

It is a fatal mistake to see the cross as the end of the road. While it may be the end of one road, it is the beginning of another. We lay down our lives for Jesus to do with them whatever he will, but then he gives us the excitement of a fresh beginning.

It is at the cross, which in Roman times stood as a symbol of darkness and defeat, that we can see the hallmarks of hope and the promise of new life. Jesus affirmed this in saying, "I tell you the truth, whoever hears my word and believes him who sent me has eternal life and will not be condemned; he has crossed over from death to life" (John 5:24). When the darkness of Good Friday descended upon Jesus, he died. In that one event God took upon himself the penalty and the punishment that was deservedly ours. My condemnation—literally, God's right to judge me—was swept away in the death of his Son (Romans 8:1)!

So what is the result? I begin to live on the far side of the cross. I know I am forgiven and God loves me. I am headed for heaven, and I can no longer be found "guilty." My sentence has been passed, yet I am acquitted because someone took my place! No wonder I cannot see the cross as a dark event, for it is where my light begins to dawn. Here Jesus died and made room for me to die also so that a divine makeover of my life could begin. What seemed to be terribly bad news can now be received as good news. Jesus' death on the cross achieves two things for us: it teaches us how to die, and it teaches us how to live.

It didn't take long for the truth to come out. Two days after the crucifixion two sorrowful disciples were walking the seven or so miles from Jerusalem to the village of Emmaus when a comforting stranger joined them. They later recalled how their hearts had been "burning within us" as this stranger walked and talked with them (Luke 24:32). When they realized the stranger was Jesus, they rushed back in the early darkness along the rocky and dangerous road to Jerusalem to tell the other disciples they had personally talked with Jesus (Luke 24:33–35). On the far side of the cross the good news breaks! Our hearts burn with excitement, and it becomes difficult to contain the wonderful announcement of what has happened.

Jesus died on a hill outside Jerusalem known as Calvary. About seven weeks later, in an upper room inside the city, the Holy Spirit came down on 120 followers of Jesus. The greatest danger facing the church today is to stop halfway between Calvary and Pentecost. I say this because of our failure to recognize the triumph of the cross and its inevitable consequences for all who trust Christ. Once we have uncovered the triumph of Christ's victory on the cross, we will allow him to set that triumph on fire in our lives.

This is life as Jesus intended for us—on the far side of the cross.

Starting a New Story

The story with which I began this chapter is one that I once struggled to tell. The conclusion was nothing short of an act of God, but our children's lives were not the only ones that changed on the far side of the cross. Ruth and I have served at our church now for a few years, and we have loved every minute of it. Previous roles with national and international organizations have contributed their own joy and pain to our lives. As president of World Relief, I literally traveled the globe, but we always believed the Lord had a chapter with a local church lined up for us in the future. And now we are living it!

Being in a New England community has provided its challenges. This is not like the southern states or California, where there is an abundance of large churches. Here the percentage of evangelical Christians is in single figures, and faith has to grow in fairly infertile soil. It took me months to realize why God placed an Englishman in New England: this region is more secular—and therefore more like the old England, where Ruth and I had spent most of our lives—than anywhere else we have encountered in the United States.

No longer do I preach in a different megachurch each week, or concentrate on the needs of the worldwide church and its ministry to the poor, or generate interest and support for a church agency—as much as I enjoyed these things. What I do now is quite refreshing. The opportunity to develop relationships, cultivate friendships, and regularly serve and minister to the same people is exciting. Thirty-five years ago I trained to do this, and now it is happening!

I serve as the team leader of multiple staff pastors and directors, with ultimate governance and direction provided by fifteen lay elders, all of whom work quite hard. Our relationships are close, so I was surprised one day when the chairman of the elders assumed a somber and distressed expression during an elder board meeting. He soberly pointed out that, after an initial surge in numbers in the first year after Ruth and I arrived, some folks were leaving the church, and not all of them because they were moving out of the area. He pointed out that some people in the church were uncomfortable with the direction of the preaching, particularly the emphasis on the crucified life. Then, on behalf of the elders, he emphasized their commitment to the direction in which we were heading. And he presented me with a book of sermons on the cross and the life that flows from it, just in case I might be in need of additional material!

Many are beginning to recognize the dangers inherent in a cultural Christianity. By this I mean the kind of Christianity in which God is essentially given lip service, and the notion of sacrifice and loss is rarely allowed to disturb our comfort zones or tranquil horizons. The reality of the Christian life is very different. Few may face the instruction to leave family behind as they change jobs or relocate. But such things are possible, especially when you begin to live on the far side of the cross.

I struggle with the term "full-time service." Is that not what Jesus has called each one of us to? We may be nurses, teachers, businesspeople, or lawyers rather than preachers. But each of us is called to live (full-time) the life of the one who died for us. To do that we must recognize that every conclusion requires a beginning. For those who would live on the far side of the cross, the cross is where we must begin. From death can come life; but dying needs to precede living. Out of our struggle to become obedient to the will of God emerges our surrender to him and then our dependence upon his life in us.

The dying comes first. Then comes life, on the far side. That is the paradox of the crucified life.

Prayer ▶ Dear Lord Jesus, if living for you means dying with you first, then please help me to learn what it means to be crucified to myself so that I may really live for you. Reveal to me the areas of my life and inner spirit that must change to make this possible. Thank you that after the crucifixion comes the resurrection. Please help me to live on the far side of the cross. Amen.

CHAPTER NINE

Broken

WARNING
– BREAKAGES MUST BE REPLACED

Most of us possess things to which we are attached. A baby may cherish a teddy bear. A preteen may have a special jacket. A young adult might be drawn to a car. And me, well, I have to confess that I do love my grandfather clock!

Perhaps I shouldn't *love* it. After all, it's only a material possession. And I have always been taught not to love something that is incapable of loving me in return. I love my wife, of course; and because Ruth bought this grandfather clock for me it has deep sentimental value. Although it's an American clock, it plays the chimes of Big Ben, a sound that I used to hear every day from my office in London. Since living in America, this clock had become a nostalgic substitute. That is, until we moved from Baltimore, Maryland, to Connecticut.

Our new home was colonial, quaint, and had ceilings that were seven feet and three inches high. Our clock was walnut, robust, and seven feet and six inches high. No one foresaw the problem until we tried to position the clock in the house and it just would not fit. Various helpful suggestions were made. Some thought the top of the clock could be cut off, and others suggested making a hole in the ceiling. But no one came up with a viable solution, so the clock was returned to the garage until further consideration.

Kent Carpenter is the kind of gifted man every church appreciates. His skills, especially in carpentry, have been invaluable to Habitat for Humanity as well as to our congregation. We first met on the afternoon of the clock fiasco. I had been assured that Kent and others would make moving into our house seem easy. The others did, but when it came to fixing door handles, putting up curtain rods, and the like, Kent had gone missing. This was strange, since Kent had been told that the new pastor was useless at anything practical, which is why Kent's wife had been swift to offer his services. But Kent was nowhere to be seen.

Four hours later Kent reemerged to tell his story. Knowing about the clock problem, he had quietly taken, without permission, five inches from the top of the wooden base of the clock (which he then added to his stock of kindling). It is little wonder that Kent, now a dear friend, is occasionally but lovingly referred to as "the executioner"!

Now the clock fits in the house, and the chimes of Big Ben ring out to mark each quarter hour. No one can identify, without help, where Kent's skilled hands made the incision. Without the removal of those five inches, the clock would still stand mute and useless in the garage. Today the clock receives great compliments, but only because Kent did a great job. His actions gave it "life" and a renewed purpose.

This is exactly what the Lord Jesus wants to do for you and for me. Each of us needs to be trimmed down to size by his loving hand, broken from what is surplus to his requirements, and made ready to fulfill the destiny he has prepared for us. All of this is impossible until we allow God to perform the necessary surgery to adapt us for his purposes and to prepare us for his service.

Giving Up on God

Throughout history, God has offered his love to those he would uniquely mold to be his people. Then comes the problem: we are reluctant to be exposed to God's discipline, let alone to his carpentry tools! We recognize that the clock should be chiming in the house rather than standing silently in the garage. Nevertheless, contemplating the pain and transformation involved in being cut down to size creates resistance within us.

Moses experienced this with the people of Israel. Their God had brought them out of Egypt, and their rescue was spectacular. As the waters of the Red Sea crashed around the heads of the pursuing Egyptian army, the Israelites could have simply released their destiny into the hands of the God who had delivered them. No way! What short memories they had. Soon their reluctance, fear, and disobedience turned an eleven-day sprint to the Promised Land into a forty-year marathon in the wilderness.

Still, their God provided them with water from a rock and food from heaven, and he kept their shoes and clothing from wearing out. Even when God's people denied his love and doubted his word, he did not give up on them. They, however, continued to give up on him.

Their rebellion was straightforward, but also subtle.

- They never refused to eat the food God provided, but they moaned about eating it.
- They never ceased worshiping God, but they added to their worship local deities, or they designed physical images to make God more culturally relevant to the surrounding people.
- They never explicitly rejected their God, but they refused to obey the leaders he provided.

Before long they resorted to grumbling and complaining. The flesh does that when it is challenged. They became resentful and bitter, which happens when people complain so much that their grumbling becomes an art form. The parallels in our own lives are obvious.

The Israelites' "fleshly" voices spoke of how they despised their leaders, conditions, lifestyle, and even God's government over them. Tragically, none of the rebels, as a result, was allowed to enter the Promised Land. Their responses were so understandable that we may feel our hearts going out to them. Conditions were difficult. The further they journeyed from Egypt, the better Egypt seemed to them. The actions and inclinations of the flesh may appear "natural" and "normal," yet that is precisely the problem. There is a danger that we will accept the lifestyle of those around us as the way we should live. Perhaps we need to examine if we sometimes conform in a convenient way to the standards of our friends, colleagues, and neighbors—just like the Israelites. They lost the Promised Land through that choice and instead had to settle for a wilderness in their future. We have been warned!

Nothing Less Than Everything

The people of Israel would not allow God to cut them down to size. They always had an excuse for their reluctance to walk with God. Sadly, this may creep into our lives. We are offered opportunities to serve God and to be involved in the ministry of his family. Yet other commitments claim priority.

Often we allow God to chip away at us, but the reality of spiritual brokenness is a no-go area. At the core, this indicates that we are trying to build our love for the Lord on the existing foundation of our lives. We struggle with the idea that he might ask us to replace who we have been with who we could become. To do that, the foundation of our old self would first need to be broken. It is when things are taken away from us that the real challenge comes.

It would be hard not to be moved listening to Joel and LeAnn tell their story. As new recruits to the elder board of the church, they were required to share with the elders and staff how God had been at work in their lives. All went well as they told of growing to love Jesus and to know him personally. The problem was that they had been part of a sectarian group that demanded exclusive rights upon their lives. Joel broke down and wept as he spoke of the challenge involved in separating themselves from that context and discovering freedom in a wider church context.

As people gathered around to pray for them, we all knew that God was at work, breaking and remolding their lives. Few of us realized how current this breaking would be. A few days after becoming an elder, Joel, who is in his thirties, learned that the position he held in a major company was no longer his. Forced relocation to another area seemed likely. Joel and LeAnn were broken again; yet determined prayer produced results. Against the odds, Joel found a new job locally, for God is at work in their lives.

One of the first worship songs I ever heard suggested that we wanted God to take us and to *break* us, that he might then shape our lives into what he intends us to be. Over time, many people began to sing the song differently, expressing the desire for God to take us and to *make* us what he wants us to be. At first glance the discrepancy may not seem significant. The distinction may appear to be a subtle one, yet there is a huge difference between the desire for God to "make" us rather than to "break" us. There is something much nicer, and less painful, about the idea that God is simply building me into something different. But as Joel and LeAnn discovered twice, brokenness is sometimes God's route for our journey.

The Necessity of Brokenness

The need to be broken is something we prefer not to accept. There is a reason for this reluctance. A deep-seated principle exists in each of us: we would prefer to live our own lives. It may sound strange and distinctly old-fashioned to call this "sin," but that is precisely what it is. None of us is exempt from it, "for all have sinned and fall short of the glory of God" (Romans 3:23).

Sin operates as a root within us and begins to produce its bitter fruit in our lives. The Pharisees had this thinking reversed. They imagined that their actions created sin, or "uncleanness." No, sin led to their actions. As Jesus said, "From within, out of men's hearts, come evil thoughts, sexual immorality, theft, murder, adultery, greed, malice, deceit, lewdness, envy, slander, arrogance and folly. All these evils come from inside and make a man 'unclean'" (Mark 7:21–23).

Cravings generated through sin are called "the flesh." This is not a reference to the human body, but to the carnal desires of our human nature. Some of our desires, such as the desires to eat and sleep, are necessary. The danger comes when self-gratification becomes our dominant focus, and the flesh and its carnal desires exercise control over our behavior. The apostle Paul says that each of us becomes a "slave to sin." "For what I want to do I do not do, but what I hate I do. . . . It is no longer I myself who do it, but it is sin living in me" (Romans 7:14–17). Paul was right: we are enslaved. The flesh rules and tries to ensure that we never admit it!

This is not what God intended; but ever since the disobedience of Adam and Eve this is what we face. That is precisely why the Lord Jesus had to come as our Savior and Deliverer. We cannot help ourselves. Even after we realize that his death has abolished our slavery, we still act as those enslaved by the flesh.

As Ruth and I walked along a beach a couple of days ago, we noticed many pieces of broken glass. Some beer bottles had been thrown into the sea to then be smashed against the rocks by the waves. We didn't realize, until we picked up a couple of pieces, that the constant action of the water and the sand had blunted the sharp edges of the shards of glass. And the water had changed the color of some of the glass, making the ugliness of a broken beer bottle into fragments of beauty. Broken lives immersed in the Holy Spirit can tell the same story.

We may assume that the role of the flesh in our lives can coexist with God's role. Let me tell you, it can't! One or the other will emerge as the victor. Only when Jesus is allowed to live and reign in our lives, in his rightful position as Lord and King, can he transform our lives into all that he wants us to be. Only then will he truly be able to show his love through us.

But to know that reality we first have to be broken. Then the Spirit of God can begin to do his transforming work on the broken pieces.

The Value of Brokenness

In the physical realm, when something becomes broken its value is reduced and its usefulness is diminished. It is intriguing that the opposite applies in the spiritual realm. There, in another paradox, brokenness creates more value than what was previously present.

Cash in the Attic, a BBC television program, has introduced millions of people to the idea that they might have hidden treasures lurking in their homes. An antiques expert is called in to search for undiscovered valuables, occasionally striking gold with a valuable painting or a piece of pottery, jewelry, or furniture. More often than not, however, he concedes, "There is evidence of some damage here." Or he might say, "There seems to have been an attempt at repair." Occasionally he will have to admit, "It appears as if these pieces have been glued together." At these words, the owner's face falls and the estimated value plummets.

That scenario is in the material world. Spiritually, an un-marked man or woman is worth far less than one who has been smashed to pieces and patiently remodeled by a loving Father. It can be argued that God can fully use only what has been broken. Jesus fed a multitude of people with five broken loaves of bread (Matthew 14:15–21). Mary of Bethany broke her alabaster jar and poured expensive perfume, worth more than a working man's annual wages, upon Jesus to prepare him for burial (Mark 14:3–9). The fragrance from this broken vessel stayed with Jesus throughout the agonies and indignities he suffered. God will never reject the offering of a broken spirit and a contrite heart in a man or woman whom he has conquered (Psalm 51:17).

As we endure brokenness, our lives are restored to God's original intention for us. God oftentimes breaks us in certain areas of our lives so that he can use us for something bigger. As we experience his hand and his transforming love in our lives, he begins to change us in ways we could never change on our own. This transformation may come at the cost of being broken, but the Lord who died for us does not smash us beyond repair. Far from it!

Ironically, when we submit a previously unyielded part of our lives to the Lord Jesus, the result is usually not despondency, but a sense of relief—the reward of joy that the Holy Spirit provides. The single most incredible breakage of all was the body of Jesus himself, crucified so we could be restored to an intimate and personal relationship with God. Yet "for the joy set before him [he] endured the cross, scorning it shame, and sat down at the right hand of the throne of God" (Hebrews 12:2).

True brokenness comes in resigning control of what we have and who we are to the God who loved us enough to die for us. That surrender is painful, but the eternal joy that follows is the exhilarating reward.

While I was leading a mission team some years ago, I watched God gently deal with a seventeen-year-old musician named Pete. As the Lord challenged Pete about his lifestyle and the depth of his love for Jesus, Pete finally broke apart. I had never seen anything quite like it. This young man was so broken by the love of God that his tears formed a puddle on the wooden floor beneath his bowed head. There was nothing superficial about that moment. The Lord stripped Pete of his calcified outer layers and laid bare the reality of his spiritual life.

It was a clash of wills. Pete finally subordinated his own will for his life to God's will for his life. Something changed that day. When you submit a part of your life that you were unwilling to submit before, you feel the weight and guilt of your sin. But then the Holy Spirit comes with his joy. For Pete, tears of sorrow borne from the Holy Spirit's irresistible grace began to turn into tears of relief and joy. Pete later got married, took a job, and settled into service in a local church. Occasionally I receive a letter from this man whose brokenness brought him into reality.

We can compromise and accept a hypocritical spiritual life that claims to be Christian yet gives little evidence of being more than play-acting. Or, like Pete in his tears, we can finally give in and accept the path of brokenness—facing up to what it means to die to ourselves and discovering the freshness and vitality of the joy God brings to our everyday lives. This is the only way we can progress into that new life that God intends for us. Like Jesus, we need to be ready and willing to be broken—not just once, but on a daily basis. We will then know, as he did, that joy will come to us for eternity.

Across the centuries, the writings and memoirs of Christians who had a profoundly deep relationship with God have revealed the principle that God cannot fully bless a person until he has first broken that person's will. Furthermore, the degree of blessing and joy we receive from God is in direct proportion not to the financial donation we provide to a "ministry," but to the completeness of the victory that the Lord Jesus gains over our lives.

Perhaps you are trying desperately to live for Jesus. Stop attempting to do it for him. Let him break the stubborn hold of self-will, and then watch as he starts to live his life *in you*. Without being broken, our lives can neither have their intended quality nor acquire their true value. But when we have been lovingly cut down to size, pruned by the master vine-dresser, then something far more beautiful emerges.

The apostle Peter wrote, "Since Christ suffered in his body, arm yourselves also with the same attitude, because he who has suffered in his body is done with sin. As a result, he does not live the rest of his earthly life for evil human desires, but rather for the will of God" (1 Peter 4:1–2). It is out of our death to our will, our brokenness to what *we* could achieve, and our emptiness in terms of human ability that our God can bring true life and real joy!

Prayer ▶ Spirit of God, please meet me in my need. Even if it means that you take me and break me, would you then mold me and fill me? Draw me toward this broken state of heart. Please rearrange my priorities to align with your will and your kingdom. Empty me of myself, and then, Lord, please use me for your glory. Amen.

CHAPTER TEN

Spirit-Filled

SCARED OF THE SPIRIT?

It was early summer in Israel. Gazing out over Galilee gave me the amazing sense that little had changed, in terms of the physical topography, since Jesus walked there two thousand years previously. Some other things had also not changed.

Twenty-six of us from the church were engaged in a spiritual retreat. This was my twelfth trip to Israel, and it was a thrill to introduce friends to places that mean so much to me—none more than this site. Eremos Heights, with its cove and symbolic pillar overlooking Galilee, is regarded by many as the "solitary place" where Jesus came to talk with his Father (Mark 1:35). It may well be the location where he preached the Sermon on the Mount. Be that as it may, it is a wonderful setting for peering into the past, contemplating Jesus, and meditating upon the future with him. I had given the group three hours for this purpose. But our time got interrupted.

The day before, we had been at the ruins of Hazor and viewed the obscenity of an eighth-century BC Asherah pole, which had been used in pagan worship. Now, on Eremos Heights, a member of our party saw an object that looked suspiciously similar. I was not particularly surprised. Israel has never totally escaped from its spiritual past. I had encountered Asherah poles littering Eremos Heights on prior trips. They had obviously been shaped and placed there in order to desecrate what for many pilgrims is a holy site. Some things just don't change. It didn't take long to identify a series of marker stones placed to designate this site for pagan worship. They had been recently created, so the intent was obvious. The only question was, What we were prepared to do about it?

Many years ago, while confronting practicing witches in a media debate on Halloween night, I had concluded that spiritual warfare was no myth. And having seen people struggle with spiritual assaults in the aftermath of removing an Asherah pole, I paused before taking action. But after a few of us got together and prayed, we decided to take action.

Young Jamie Marshall, who was my intern that summer, boldly stepped forward to pull up the first stone. Jamie had developed his muscles and was a bit proud of his strength. He pulled, pushed, and tugged, but there was no way that the stone would move.

Jamie seemed a little startled when I offered to help. One look at my physique was likely enough to persuade him that there was little I could do. Sure enough, when I took a try, the stone did not budge. Then I began to call for help: "Not by might, nor by power, but by your Spirit, Lord." The rock moved. Soon it was unearthed and discarded.

Jamie then attempted to dislodge the next rock, again with similar results. Only when he verbalized the need for the power of God's Spirit could he remove these instruments of pagan worship.

Time and again God longs to show us that when human resources fail he is ready to be there for us. His Spirit comes to our rescue when we experience failure via our own strength. If only we would surrender earlier and recognize that a crucified life provides opportunity for God to work in and through us.

Losing Control

We may want to panic when we recognize that the spiritual life cannot be lived under our control. We will encounter circumstances that defy human explanation. There will be situations that we cannot resolve alone. There is also a power, the power of the Holy Spirit, that God places in our lives in order to make us different.

It may be easier, naturally, to wrap our minds around a Father revealed in creation or a Son who walked in history. The activities of the Holy Spirit are intangible and might impact our lives in the future in ways we cannot anticipate. Some people feel more comfortable looking backward to what the Lord Jesus has done for us. By contrast, it can seem more difficult to understand an indefinable force that comes to live within us, or a God who calls us to victories but fails to explain how he intends to achieve them. After all, who knows what the Holy Spirit might do?

It is this kind of fear, or innate reservation, that can stop us from moving forward in God. There should be little surprise that after the crucifixion a bunch of frightened disciples could only be transformed into world-changing followers of Jesus by receiving power from on high. Jesus had promised his disciples, "I will not leave you as orphans; I will come to you" (John 14:18). He reassured them that his going away would be to their advantage (John 16:7). Instead of walking alongside them, Jesus' Spirit would live within them. Sometimes I wonder if they were really convinced by this argument. We can be the same: we can start out courageously in our relationship with God only to come to an abrupt stop. What is it that causes me to be frightened of moving into the unknown with him? Why are we reluctant to begin the great adventure of moving forward into all that he has for us? What brings us to a sudden halt? Or is it just me?

Perhaps we are reluctant to understand that God does not want us to live alone, striving to follow him through our own abilities. He wants to provide us with resources beyond our comprehension. He offers to fill us with his Holy Spirit, so that we can live his life through the power of his presence in us.

Unfortunately, the idea of losing control of our lives and encountering supernatural power has frightened many believers into resisting God's Spirit. It is one thing to be sold out to God, but it is another to allow him to win the victories through us that he intends, especially when we no longer control the means by which he operates.

Scripture tells how King Jehoash of Israel paid the prophet Elisha an unexpected visit when Elisha was on his deathbed. The king's flattering words didn't impress the dying prophet, who immediately instructed Jehoash to shoot an arrow out the window. Elisha announced that this was a prophetic sign representing the Lord's "arrow of victory" over Aram (or Syria), Israel's enemy (2 Kings 13:17).

Elisha then urged Jehoash to take the rest of the arrows and strike the ground with them. The king's response was halfhearted, as he struck the ground three times. This made Elisha angry, and he said, "You should have struck the ground five or six times; then you would have defeated Aram and completely destroyed it. But now you will defeat it only three times" (2 Kings 13:19).

Elisha knew that Jehoash's lack of faith and zeal was throwing away the victories that God could have given Israel. The prophet died; and, sure enough, the Arameans continued to oppress Israel until Jehoash finally recovered some ground by defeating the Arameans three times (2 Kings 13:20–25).

To understand this story, we need to know the historical and the political situation. Israel, at the time, was threatened by the strongest military force they had faced since entering Canaan. The nation of Assyria posed a major threat to Israel's survival. Israel's national security had remained intact because to the northeast—between Assyria and Israel—lay her old enemy Aram. As long as Aram served as a buffer state, Israel was safe. Jehoash knew that the number of times he beat the ground with the arrows represented the number of times the Lord's "arrow of victory" would beat the Arameans in battle. A couple of times would be sweet revenge for past defeats. But more than three times could threaten an Aramean collapse, which would bring Israel face-to-face with the enormous military might of Assyria. Faced with this sobering challenge, King Jehoash took the coward's way out and stopped after three times (2 Kings 13:18). No wonder Elisha was furious. The king would not rely on God to direct and protect his people.

Are we any braver today? There may be times when we are afraid to go out on a limb with God to discover where he wants to take us. We may even be secretly scared of what his Holy Spirit wants to do in and through our lives.

God doesn't just want to give us a feeling; he wants to give us his own Spirit. He challenges us to do exploits in his name—not through our power, but through his.

Stop—We Have Not Been Properly Introduced!

It's understandable to be cautious about beginning a journey when you are uncertain about the identity and the character of your traveling companion. This is how some of us feel about the Holy Spirit.

A woman took me aside recently and asked me to confirm that nothing supernatural would ever take place in our church. I apologized for being unable to give her that assurance! In view of the almighty God, the idea that he should deny his own nature in order to accommodate our fears seems faintly ridiculous.

Considering that the Holy Spirit is "supernatural" by definition, there is nothing particularly unusual, odd, or strange about the way he works. But there is nothing human about how he works, either, because the Holy Spirit is God himself. Are we to be afraid of the God who 366 times in the Bible urges people not to be afraid? We don't need to fear his nature, his Spirit, or where he will take us.

Scripture reveals that the Holy Spirit is personal, just as the Father and the Son are personal. To put it plainly, the Holy Spirit is God's presence in us. He is so personal that

- He feels (Ephesians 4:30).
- He acts (John 16:7–11).
- He knows (John 14:26).

The Spirit does all this for a purpose. He takes hold of regular people who have surrendered their lives to God and makes us into change agents in our world. He begins to mold us into those who will transform the future of the world and the population of heaven.

One person who desired this to happen was Bill Bright, the founder of Campus Crusade for Christ. He pointed out that when a Christian is filled with the Holy Spirit, he or she is filled with Jesus Christ. So the Christian no longer thinks of Christ as one who helps us do some kind of Christian task, but rather he thinks of Christ as the one who does the work through the Christian.

Since he is God, the Holy Spirit can be everywhere simultaneously, molding ordinary people into the likeness of the Lord they love and serve. As we grow, he reveals areas in our lives where we need to be strengthened. He acts like a potter who flicks the rim of a pot and listens to discern a perfect glaze. If the tone is wrong, then he puts us back into God's furnace until the fire has done its work. Only then can the Holy Spirit release us to live and act as the hands and feet of Jesus.

Stop—We May Not Be in Control!

A close friend of mine was speaking at a large Christian conference, trying to challenge a group of local church leaders about the role of the Holy Spirit in their churches. He suggested that if the Holy Spirit were removed from our congregations it might be possible for approximately 95 percent of our church activities to continue on unchanged. It would appear to be "business as usual."

He intended this to be a daring statement, designed to provoke a strong declaration from the church leaders about how the Holy Spirit was alive and well—highly active in the churches represented by the group. My friend was greatly disconcerted that the one question raised at the end of the session came from a church leader who wanted to know how a congregation could be structured to cover the remaining 5 percent! In this leader's mind, the intervention of the Holy Spirit was too unpredictable to be included. He was more comfortable with what could be controlled.

The desire to stick to known territory is what provides the motivation for this safety-first policy. We deeply desire to feel in control. The idea that the Holy Spirit might take us where he wants or work in us as he wants makes us distinctly cautious. Why are we wary of the one who is the essence of God working in our lives? That is a good question, especially when the most subversive thing he is trying to do is to make us more like Jesus!

There is an answer that may shake our security system. "An enemy has done this. . . . Satan has opposed the doctrine of the Spirit-filled life about as bitterly as any other doctrine there is. He has confused it, opposed it and surrounded it with false notions and fears. He has blocked every effort of the church of Christ to receive from the Father, his divine and blood-bought patrimony [or inheritance]. The church has tragically neglected this great liberating truth—that there is now for the child of God a full and wonderful and completely satisfying anointing with the Holy Spirit."[1]

Some people feel most comfortable aligning themselves with a particular movement or a set of beliefs within the faith. Others, however, have begun to emphatically reject labels, whatever they might be, in their quest for the living God. Frankly, we can no longer afford the luxury of supporting a particular Christian "team" or "party." Instead, we must seek the fullness of the Holy Spirit *wherever* God is to be found. Scripture provides us with invaluable guidance to discern the presence of the Holy Spirit. We are urged to always "test the spirits to see whether they are from God" (1 John 4:1). "The spirits" refers to people who are motivated by a spirit, whether by the Holy Spirit or an evil spirit. We always need to make sure that it is God, not a human or evil spirit, at work. Then we can join in.

---

1. A. W. Tozer, *How to Be Filled with the Holy Spirit* (Camp Hill, PA: Christian Publications, Inc., 2001), 32.

We are instructed to be filled with the Holy Spirit (Ephesians 5:18). So let's ask ourselves, *Where would I be today without the Holy Spirit in my life?* I hope we don't have to admit that, due to neglecting the Spirit, there would be no difference in our lives. If this is the case, we are still desperately trying to determine our own direction. Jesus explained that the Holy Spirit is like the wind: it "blows wherever it pleases" (John 3:8). If we are still eager to retain control of our lives, we will be reluctant to allow the Spirit to take us where he wants.

The Holy Spirit has been called many things. He has been referred to as Satan's unsolved problem. He has been identified as the author of every positive revolution in the history of the church and society. Appropriately he has been described as God's secret weapon, bringing explosive life to his people. Whatever way you look at it, Jesus promised that the Holy Spirit would be the reality of the presence of the living God at home in our hearts, revealing Jesus in the lives of every believer.

What causes our fear of the Holy Spirit? The answer lies in a sense of uncertainty about where the Holy Spirit might take us, although he will always act in line with the biblical pattern.

The Holy Spirit draws us to the cross and then takes us to the far side of the cross by equipping and enabling us to lead surrendered lives in the way that our God always intended. When our old self has died, then the Holy Spirit can come and make all things new (Romans 8:13–14). That is what is meant by "the crucified life." When we acknowledge our inability to do the will of God, we finally surrender to the Holy Spirit.

Where the Spirit Blows

The twenty-first century will probably see more Christian martyrs than all previous centuries combined have seen. This was true of the twentieth century as well, and the situation is deteriorating in much of the world. Yet many people today want a faith that can be comfortably added to their daily routine. The church often reflects the culture of its society. Far from the church changing the world, the world is sculpting the church.

Others are far less satisfied with the current state of affairs. They are asking how a church can develop an authentic combination of healing, deliverance from demons, prayer, and submission to the authority of Scripture. How can we grow to resemble the early church, where all of these spiritual expressions were valued? No group claimed a monopoly on the Holy Spirit, but each saw him at work among them in diverse ways.

One might even ponder, *Where would I find the Holy Spirit changing people's lives in such a dramatic fashion today?* The answer is that you can see God at work, building his church in this way, in many parts of the world. In Cambodia and Mozambique, in Albania and Nicaragua, in Ethiopia and Iraq—wherever the church has been under pressure, its true character has shone through.

One notable place is an Assemblies of God church in Tehran. Several hundred people attend this thriving fellowship in the capital city of Iran. The congregation boldly advertises its presence with a large metal cross attached to the front of the church building, elevated so that no one can miss it.

One Friday (the Muslim day of worship), a blind eighty-six-year-old man tapped his way past the gates of the church. He paused and asked some of those nearby if this was the church. They attempted to redirect him to the mosque because they were sure that must be his intended destination. Imagine their surprise when he told them that while praying for his village he had seen an image of a great white cloud descending upon it—and in the center of the cloud was the vivid outline of a cross. That was the reason he searched for the church. Discovering that Jesus was the way God intended to help his village, he surrendered his life to his newly discovered Savior.

When asked how far he had traveled to find the church, his answer was astounding. At eighty-six years of age, he had journeyed by bus and on foot about 850 kilometers (530 miles). Now he tries to make the journey once a month, just to be able to worship with brothers and sisters in Jesus.

God is not at work solely in the Middle East. While visiting a seminary in Delhi, North India, recently, I conducted a survey. One of the questions focused on the factors that led the students to come to faith in Christ. I asked them to add any reason that was not on the survey. Thirty-four of the 155 students responded that their personal experience of healing was a major factor in bringing them to Christ. One young man training for ministry wrote these amazing words: "I saw my brother raised from the dead and gave my life to Jesus." Well, what else would you do?! Five other students had also personally witnessed a resurrection.

As a basic part of the Christianity they had embraced, most of the students had prayed for freedom from either witchcraft or demonic assault, for physical healing and protection, and for miraculous provision of what they needed to serve God. For them, a faith devoid of any supernatural element would be incomprehensible.

A few years ago, I was one of the speakers at the missions weekend of a church in southern California, a large congregation known for its commitment to global outreach. In a preparatory briefing, I was staggered to be asked if I would "Go easy on miracles."

To the vast number of people who have come to faith through visions or dreams, to the African witch doctor who has witnessed the God who does greater things, and to the beleaguered and oppressed Christian minorities in Muslim nations, such as the Balkans, such a comment would be unfathomable.

Set on Fire

A crucified life—anywhere in the world—is not prepared to stand still. Our journey is from the cross to the Spirit, and if we fail to move on, it is at our peril. Tragically, the desire to stay in charge can leave us becalmed, stuck halfway between Good Friday and Pentecost. We have arrived at a point of initial surrender to Jesus Christ, yet we struggle to let go of control. Too many of us are trying to operate our lives with our *finite* power, when God is ready to release his *infinite* power within us.

God's Spirit comes to set our lives ablaze with a new radiance and power. He does not urge us, in our own strength, to more truly love God and the things that God loves. No, the

Spirit comes to work through us—as he did through Stephen, the first Christian martyr—to:

- Serve others (Acts 6:1–6).
- Live powerfully (Acts 6:8).
- Speak boldly (Acts 7:51–60).

This is wonderfully fulfilling. What more could we want?

Jim Elliot, a twentieth-century martyr, wrote in his journal, "Psalm 104:4: 'He makes His ministers a flame of fire.' Am I ignitable? God deliver me from the dread asbestos of 'other things.' Saturate me with the oil of the Spirit that I may be a flame." This amazing power of the Holy Spirit to burn up the old and set us on fire to live for Jesus is available to all of God's people.

The Spirit doesn't come to fulfill our personal desires or ambitions. He comes to be in the driver's seat! He comes to conform our lives to his purposes for us and—like an eternal Olympic torch—to keep the Spirit's fire burning within us!

Stop, I Don't Want to Go There!

For King Jehoash, the rubber had hit the road. He thought, *I won't beat the arrows on the ground too many times. If I do, then only God will be left between Israel and the armies of Assyria.* He might as well have thought *I don't have the faith for that* or *I'm just too scared to go there.*

If we were brutally honest with ourselves, we might acknowledge that we are content to stay where we are. We are delighted when God blesses us. We are thrilled to see minor victories on our journey. But the idea of an unrestricted journey from the sacrifice of the cross to the ignition of the combustible Spirit within us . . . Well, isn't that taking it a little bit too far? And didn't we receive all that we need at conversion anyway?

No one can doubt that we receive the Holy Spirit when we surrender our lives to the Lord Jesus. But is that the end of our journey? If he comes into our lives at conversion, then there must be enough evidence of his presence to prove the fact. The famed twentieth-century British preacher David Martyn Lloyd-Jones voiced a concern about the reality of the Holy Spirit in our lives when he exclaimed, "Got it, got it—well, where is it, I ask?"

The simple truth is that each of us needs to know an *ongoing* work of the Holy Spirit in our hearts and lives. If you and I want to be filled to overflowing with the love and power of the living God, then we first need to be emptied. We need to lose our fears and trust him. It all begins at the cross. But that work then needs to continue.

When the nineteenth-century American evangelist D. L. Moody was asked why he needed a continual filling of the Holy Spirit, his response was a masterpiece of spiritual common sense. He said, "I need to be filled with the Spirit every moment of each day because I leak." We too can be very leaky people—people who need to know the reality of God's present activity in our experience of him *today*, not just in our memories. We were never destined to simply sit apart from the crowd or to just limp our way through life. The Holy Spirit provides what is lacking in our spiritual lives so that we may be fully effective for God.

God will not lead all of us the same way. He knows how different each of his children is in their temperaments, responses, and needs. God leads us in different ways but toward the same destination. He may give you a mighty and loud encounter with the Holy Spirit, or he may lead you into a quiet but ongoing engagement with the sanctifying work of his Spirit within you.

Something interesting happened when my wife prayed for a married couple on one occasion. The husband was a quiet, steady kind of person. The wife had a more effervescent personality. Together they asked the Holy Spirit to flood through every area of their lives—not to be confined, but to overflow. Ruth then watched as the bubbly wife became silent before her Lord, while the quiet husband became outwardly joyful.

On another occasion, I prayed for a lady whose husband wanted nothing to do with what we were doing. She received a quiet touch from God; he burst into tongues for the first time in his life.

You may speak in tongues, or you may not. You may have a spectacular "crisis" encounter with God, or you may not. You may be visibly transformed, or you may remain externally much the same. You may worship God by murmuring your love to him in your own language, or you may find another language replacing your own. Paul urges us not to put too much emphasis in the wrong place (1 Corinthians 14:18–19). Don't get hung up on the experiences. God works differently in each of us. The common ground lies in the way he opens a doorway to a new dimension of living. We are called to pursue what he gives us, not what he doesn't. We are called to journey with him as he provides stepping stones from merely knowing about God to truly knowing him at work in our lives.

We have an enemy who will do everything in his power to prevent this from happening. Satan tries to foster opposition within us to the idea that we can actually *know* God rather than just intellectually *know about* him. The ministry of the Holy Spirit is to bring our hearts into a personal, intimate, vibrant, unfolding relationship with God. The task of our enemy is to encourage us to always settle for second best. God wants us to be filled to overflowing with his Spirit, for those who have been emptied do need to be filled.

This Holy Spirit, God himself, longs to be a living, exciting reality in our lives—a real person, known and loved—and not considered as some mere force out there. That may work for *Star Wars*, but it is never sufficient for the crucified life. For what begins at the cross finds its fullness in the Holy Spirit.

Prayer ▶ Holy Spirit, would you strip me of my fear of the unknown? Would you empty me of everything that does not reflect Jesus in my life? Reveal yourself within me in a way that I have never known before. I want to go much, much deeper with you. I want to sense a personal relationship connecting us. Please fill my life with your Holy Spirit to overflowing so that I may radiate the love of Jesus . . . again . . . and again . . . and again. For the glory of Jesus, Amen.

CHAPTER ELEVEN

Fruit

FOR HIS GLORY

Where the Jordan River empties into the Dead Sea is the lowest place on earth. It is also bare, barren, and empty. The whole area is synonymous with salt. Tourists descend on spas for baths and beauty treatments and the opportunity to float in the super-buoyant waters of the Dead Sea.

One of my colleagues has an unusual claim to fame. Unaware of the special properties of the water, he once took a running dive into the Dead Sea. Fortunately he lived to tell the tale, but the experience goes down as one of the least pleasant and most painful of his life.

Driving into the Jordan Valley leads you toward Jericho, considered by many to be the oldest city in the world. Today Jericho is firmly under Palestinian control, but much of the pace of life and the local activities are reminiscent of the days when the local chief tax collector, Zacchaeus, climbed into a tree to see Jesus.

Today, as it has for centuries, a spring of water bubbles in the heart of the city. It is the prime source of Jericho's natural beauty and fertility. Nearly three thousand years ago Elisha stood at this very spring and confronted a major civic crisis. Some five hundred years earlier the Israelites had entered the Promised Land. The first city that God led them to capture, and destroy, was Jericho. As a way of demonstrating that the conquered land belonged to the Lord, Joshua pronounced a curse upon the person who would attempt to rebuild Jericho (Joshua 6:26). The city had recently been rebuilt, with difficulty (1 King 16:34). But apparently the water was still under Joshua's curse, causing both the land and the people much suffering.

The citizens enjoyed living in a place famous for being "pleasant" or "well situated" (2 Kings 2:19). The beauty was there to be admired, but it was always short-lived. Blossoms swiftly faded and leaves fell. Young, tender shoots of wheat shriveled and died. Just when it was about to ripen, the fruit dropped off the tree, and the harvest that had so much potential came to nothing. It was "Jericho fruit"; it never managed to live up to its initial promise. Year after year the people of Jericho watched their crops in the hope that this time something would be different. Nothing changed. Every year the animals miscarried, the land was unproductive, and the ground was barren—all because the water was polluted.

Jericho had a serious problem that would not go away. The people were dependent on the water of their natural spring, but it was corrupted. Elisha asked the people for a bowl filled with salt. Then he threw the salt into the spring and proclaimed, "This is what the Lord says: 'I have healed this water. Never again will it cause death or make the land unproductive'" (2 Kings 2:20–21). At that moment God provided the solution, and the water was purified (2 Kings 2:22).

The miraculous effects upon the land resulting from this single event were enough to remove Joshua's curse and permanently transform a community. That water still remains pure today, and lasting fruit is naturally produced. Where would Jericho be now if it had not been for the prophet, the salt, and an act of God?

Living for His Glory

Talk of reversing curses and transforming communities may sound well out of our league. It must have felt that way for Elisha too. The simple truth is that the living God does not want us to attempt to do his work for him. What he does want, however, is for us to allow him to work through us.

When we as a congregation were grappling with the enormity of this concept, one of our pastors quietly pointed out that this was not an attempt at self-aggrandizement or ego boosting, but simply a desire to live for God's glory. Was that not what he always intended?

This short, sharp dose of spiritual reality was really helpful. Those words—"for his glory"—were a great reminder that the real purpose the Lord Jesus has for us as saved sinners is not just to preserve the freedom he won for us or to supply us with every personal benefit or spiritual present our hearts could desire. No, he wants to make us into world-changers. He blesses us so that we might become his means of bringing blessings to others. In fact, the greatest miracle of all is that he wants us to bless him in this way. This is a genuine two-way relationship!

Christ offered himself as a once-for-all sacrifice to cover our sins. And now he wants us to become "living sacrifices" (Romans 12:1) and "a holy priesthood, offering spiritual sacrifices acceptable to God through Jesus Christ" (1 Peter 2:5). We are here to bear fruit for Jesus, bringing our sacrifices to the Lord. We can give back to him from what he has first given to us.

What a purpose, what a privilege, and what a problem! We might feel more comfortable with a God who receives from us. Acts of self-sacrifice or human kindness are all very well, because that is, after all, the nature of religion. The heartbeat of authentic Christianity, however, is not these good works. The true Christian life has never consisted of what *we* do for God. It has always been about what *he* does in us and through us. His marvelous work in us can defy our human imagination.

The wonderful truth is that he comes to live and work in the hearts and lives of very ordinary people.

Jim is one of the most lovable characters you could ever hope to meet. We call him the Energizer Bunny because, like the advertising mascot for Energizer batteries, he never stops. Jim, who is an elder in our church, has voluntarily decided to limit his work involvement to the level necessary for he and his wife, Janice, to survive. He dedicates the rest of his time to the service of Jesus. As a motivator, encourager, supporter, and friend, Jim has set an incredible example.

A while back we learned that Jim's mother had died. Some of us made the journey to the church where the funeral service was to take place. There were wonderful tributes paid to her memory. The major eulogy was given by a man who began by acknowledging his surprise at being asked—"because we all know that Jim is the spiritual one in the family."

I was disappointed that Jim was not going to speak, because I knew the truth of Jim's mom's last days. He and the family had given so much in love and care, but Jim had another gift in store for her. A few days before she died, Jim led his mother to give her life to Jesus.

After fifty-plus years of marriage, Jim's father took the loss of his dear wife very hard. Again the family rallied together, giving him tremendous support.

Only a few months later, we were all back in the same church, this time to attend the funeral service for Jim's dad. This time Jim gave the eulogy. Jim eloquently thanked the family for all they had done. He expressed his gratitude to his father for a lifetime of love and support. Then he gave thanks that he and Janice had surrendered their lives to Jesus back in 1985.

You could have heard a pin drop. Jim spoke of introducing his mom to Jesus shortly before she died. Then he talked about his dad's last days. He shared what it had meant to tell his father about how his mother had found faith. Then he spoke of how his dad had come to Jesus too.

When he concluded, the church erupted into spontaneous applause. As I affirmed Jim afterwards, he quietly confessed that his father had made him promise that he would tell the story at the funeral.

More than twenty years of seemingly unfruitful witnessing were culminated, at the end, with the dawning knowledge that God was at work in the lives of Jim's parents. Together they will share eternity. The lives of Jim and Janice certainly produced late, great fruit.

Fruit-Bearing for Beginners

Our fruit-bearing introduces questions that must be asked, questions such as *What kind of fruit am I producing—and how much is it worth?* If I am brutally honest with myself, I would have to confess that too much of what I have to give is contaminated "Jericho fruit." For many people, the fruitfulness that appears to be just around the corner never emerges. Sometimes the fruit is just late in arriving.

When those looking in from the outside see the blossom, they predict fruit. They can see the potential, but they don't realize that the life-source, the water, has been corrupted, because we have placed our own efforts before what God can do. Too often it is my glory, not his glory, that is viewed in operation.

We assume that our abilities provide the life-source that God requires. Instead, we need the reality check of a forgotten truth: It is the God of peace alone who can "equip you with everything good for doing his will" and "work in us what is pleasing to him, through Jesus Christ" (Hebrews 13:20–21). God wants to be the source. Too often we fall into the trap of believing that he expects us to produce fruit on our own, so we mobilize all our efforts to achieve that objective. How dreadfully sad and unnecessary!

Have you ever driven past an orchard? As you gaze on rows of carefully cultivated fruit trees, do you see first one row and then another groaning and straining to produce fruit? Of course not. Try to imagine trunks, branches, and blossoms of each tree struggling to produce what it was created to do. The idea may seem ridiculous, but no more so than faithful Christians trying to manufacture what a loving God wants to produce within them. A fruit tree, properly cared for, will effortlessly produce fruit. When we evade God's natural work in us and resort to human effort, we end up with bitter disappointment coupled with a reluctance to admit how little fruit we have produced in our hearts and lives.

This picture may be too accurate for comfort. Sincere Christians endure the heartbreak of watching spiritual fruit grow in their lives until, just as it is about to ripen and fulfill the purpose for which it was created, the fruit falls to the ground before its time. The problem is not that we grew the wrong kind of fruit. Apple trees do not produce bananas without a major genetic change. The problem is the absence of our longing to present a life lived for his glory alone. Ian Thomas observed, "The fruit that has appeared to others has fallen—oh, so often, so *cruelly* often—to the ground—premature, immature—only to rot and never to reproduce."[1] Sure, we know what we should be. We know what we want to be. We know the Christian language, and we speak it well. But somehow we never achieve what we long to be.

This lack of achievement is not hypocrisy; it is spiritual failure. What fruit we do produce can too frequently be immature and without seed, incapable of reproducing. Sad to say, many of us can find this state of affairs pretty easy to apply to ourselves. We live with a lurking sense of doubt that we can ever become all that the Lord Jesus intended us to be. We have failed, and now we are simply tired.

But that is only our side of the story.

Decoration or Death?

Back in the 1970s I decided, like many other people, to wear a cross around my neck. I didn't want to wear a crucifix, since Jesus is no longer on the cross. So I chose a large silver cross and wore it outside of my shirt or sweater where it was visible. I saw it as a constant reminder that my life had been bought with a price.

Alan, a businessman in the clothing industry, really admired my cross. So I wasn't surprised when one day he proudly displayed his own equally large and visible cross. Because he felt Jesus' cross was immeasurably too valuable for silver, Alan purchased his cross in gold. He wanted to affirm the incredible value of the single most significant act in the whole of human history: the

---

1. W. Ian Thomas, *The Saving Life of Christ* (Grand Rapids: Zondervan, 1988), 30 (italics in original).

death of Jesus Christ on a cross—the purchase price God paid to buy Alan back for himself. He also reasoned that a gold cross symbolized the doorway to a future crown of gold.

Wearing a cross is like wearing a wedding ring: both make statements that need to be backed up by a lifestyle. Alan was asked a lot of questions about his cross, which gave him great opportunities to share his love for Jesus. At the same, however, I was becoming increasingly uncomfortable with my own cross. I eventually laid the silver cross aside and purchased a wooden one instead. I knew that I, along with many others, was beginning to take the cross for granted. It had become a nominal statement of a genuine faith.

We know that Aaron's staff produced "fruit" (buds, blossoms, and almonds), much to the consternation of the Israelites (Numbers 17:1–13). To understand the cross of Jesus as the means to produce spiritual fruit may likewise seem bizarre. Yet Jesus insists that we are here to bear fruit, not through our own efforts, but through his life in us (John 15:1–5). We are to be like a tree planted by streams of water, delighting in God and meditating on his truth; we draw nourishment from outside ourselves so all that we do prospers because of God's grace in us (Psalm 1:1–3). This is possible because of the cross, making the message of the cross not just good news, but great news!

For one grain of wheat to generate more grains, the seed must die so that others might live. The famed British preacher, Alan Redpath, used to ask the scorching question, "Tell me in the light of the cross, isn't it a scandal that you and I live today as we do?"[2] The cross of Christ and the crucified life that it engenders in me are more about the fruit-bearing that results than about anything I may receive. And when we see the results of that cross—both in us and through us—our hearts can break out in a song of surprise, echoing the words of the hymn writer who discovered that

> Bearing shame and scoffing rude,
> In my place condemned He stood;
> Sealed my pardon with His blood.
> Hallelujah! What a Savior!
>
> ("'Man of Sorrows,' What a Name,"
> by Philip P. Bliss)

Perhaps we have a natural modesty, or perhaps we have a natural failure to understand the incredible difference that a life can make when lived "in Jesus." But either way we are too often guilty of minimizing the impact that our lives could bring to our community, the fruit we could produce for his glory. When we transfer our lives to Jesus, there can be amazing results.

When the religious leaders of the day saw the courage of Peter and John and the confident way they shared their faith, they recognized that these men had been with Jesus (Acts 4:13). We, too, can be different. And what then if we are?

Only what we offer to God that comes from Jesus can have permanent value. The presence of Jesus is the antidote to "Jericho fruit." That which emanates from Jesus at work in us has eternal

---

2. Alan Redpath, quoted in Leonard Ravenhill, *Why Revival Tarries* (Minneapolis: Bethany, 1987), 56.

value. When he lives and operates through us, we will act as "salt": providing both flavoring and preservation in our world. And this saltiness will last (Matthew 5:13; Mark 9:50).

So was the problem with Jericho an absence of water? No. The people had their spring, but it produced the wrong kind of water. If our fruit is substandard, the same is never true of what Jesus brings to birth in us. When we learn to depend on his work in us for our fruitfulness, rather than on our own efforts on his behalf, the difference is amazing. The good news is that the Lord Jesus promised that if we remain in him we will be fruitful; and just as a branch draws its nourishment and strength from a vine, so we can receive all that we need from him (John 15:4). Like a tree planted along a riverbank, we will have plenty of water to draw from, and we will never fail to deliver good fruit (Psalm 1:3).

Jesus pointed out that people can be recognized for who they are by the fruit they bear (Matthew 7:15–20). We may not be responsible for the lives of others, but we are clearly accountable for our own. A healthy apple tree does not produce stunted apples. We have no excuse for producing bitter fruit or no fruit at all. When Jesus is allowed to live in and through us we discover a God who still generates earthquakes today.

Prayer ▶ Lord, I am beginning to recognize that what this world needs is more of what you can give rather than what I can provide. I am sick and tired of bearing fruit that is not pleasing to you or that interferes with the work you want to do in me. May I decrease so that you can increase and bear fruit for eternity. In Jesus, Amen.

CHAPTER TWELVE

Destiny

DON'T WASTE YOUR LIFE

She was weeping, and she was slowly dying. The tubercular cough that wracked her body signaled that there wasn't much time left—perhaps two or three years at the most—and then she would be gone. Looking at her there in the squalid hut she called home, I thought she would do well to survive for that long.

As her face contorted in pain again, Jennifer coughed and coughed. Her body was so emaciated that she resembled a concentration camp victim. Her black skin seemed to have withered during her illness. She just seemed so incredibly fragile.

We were near Nairobi, in Ongata Rongai: one of Kenya's largest slums. Here the sights and sounds of dying people were not unusual. As the lines of little huts stretched for miles into the distance, the pall of death hung permanently in the air above them.

Jennifer, however, was different. Despite all her suffering, she retained vivacity and a sense of joy that went way beyond raw courage. As we sat together on the mud floor, Jennifer started to tell me her story. She had been brought up going to church, though her belief in Jesus was contained more in her mind than in her heart. She lived pretty much the same way as everyone else, but she reckoned that was acceptable since she had Jesus.

Time passed, and as a young adult Jennifer looked for a husband. She found one in the church. Eight years later there were still no children. Within the African culture, barrenness represented disaster; and Jennifer's marriage ended in divorce. From a spiritual viewpoint, she felt that was all right. After all, she still went to church.

The next chapter of Jennifer's life involved economic hardship, and she turned to prostitution to survive. Three children were born as the result of one liaison after another. She is unable to tell any of them the identity of their father. Jennifer's downward spiral finally reached the bottom with her arrival at Ongata Rongai. There, girls sold their bodies for twenty-five to thirty cents a time.

As she related her sad saga, Jennifer wept. Throughout this period of her life, she continued to go to church and to believe in Jesus. Jennifer confessed, through her tears, that her belief was academic rather than life-transforming—and therefore nothing changed for her. That is, until the fateful day of the HIV test.

After an extreme bout of illness, she discovered that she was living with AIDS.

Finally faced with the truth of where her life had brought her, Jennifer realized that going to church was not enough. It was during those days of personal agony, realizing that her time on earth was so limited, that at last she surrendered her life to Jesus Christ. Now she weeps, not because she has found Jesus, but for the wasted years. In her head, Jennifer had known that this Jesus was "the way and the truth and the life" (John 14:6), but she had never allowed him to bring to her that life, truth, and direction.

In her surrender, Jesus brought Jennifer life-changing power, and she could not wait to tell others about him. She just naturally radiates an infectious sense of joy. It is not surprising that this lady uses every available moment to share her love for Jesus with her neighbors, hoping that they will surrender their destiny to him too.

Again the tubercular cough wracked her frail body. The tears flowed freely as she pleaded with me to carry her message to the church in the Western world: "Please tell my brothers and sisters not to live as I did; please tell them not to waste their lives." She warns that we should give our lives to Jesus when we are healthy, not when we are sick, so that the best days of our lives may be lived for him. God has a special purpose for each of his children.

Jennifer longs that we might learn from her mistakes. In her own case, she is so sorry that all she can give to the Lord are the shattered fragments of a broken life. Yet God can still use broken fragments. And soon she will be home.

Forgiveness . . . for Today *and* Tomorrow

This depth of self-examination is unpleasant and real. Many of us would be uncomfortable if others were intimately aware of our past—and perhaps even of who we are today. Although we may not be able to relate to what Jennifer experienced, we still know the realities of sin and personal failure. One of the great agonies of life is disappointment with ourselves. A personal inventory of past choices may only deepen our sense of regret and increase our yearning for true forgiveness.

It is one thing for us to know—in theory—that the crucified love of Jesus brings his forgiveness to our lives. But what does that mean? Is it similar to the way a parent offers forgiveness and reconciliation to a child, while retaining knowledge of that child's true nature? Or is it more than that?

The Bible assures us that God is totally aware of what we are really like. He inspired the apostle Paul to write to the believers in Ephesus, "As for you, you were dead in your transgressions and sins" (Ephesians 2:1). However, he also made the ultimate sacrifice in order to deliver to us this glorious possibility: "When you were dead in your sins and in the uncircumcision of your sinful nature, God made you alive with Christ" (Colossians 2:13).

Then God takes it one step further: "He forgave us all our sins" (Colossians 2:13). This incredible truth is woven through the whole fabric of the good news that Jesus brought. It was part of

- God's character (Psalm 103:1–3; 130:3–4).
- John's preparation for Jesus (Luke 3:1–3).
- The teachings of Jesus (Matthew 6:14).
- The message of the church (Acts 2:36–38).

Those first-century Christians had confidence in the absolute truth of divine forgiveness. They knew that this came *from* Jesus (Acts 5:31), *in* Jesus (Ephesians 1:7), and *through* Jesus (Acts 13:38).

A Case of Divine Amnesia

The blood of Jesus achieved the possibility and potential for forgiveness (Hebrews 9:11–22). This promised gift did not relate to forgiveness for *Christ's* sins, because there weren't any. Jesus' promise was that his sacrifice would bring forgiveness for your sins and my sins! Jesus rose from the dead and defeated death—the ultimate enemy—so that, as poor mortals dead in our sins, we could rise too.

This is the incredible wonder of the forgiveness that Jesus brings. But there is still more! God does not pretend that we have never sinned, nor will he ignore our guilt. However, he does not want us to dwell on our sins. When our sin is confessed to God, appropriate restitution is made where necessary; and then he remembers our sins no more (Jeremiah 31:34; Hebrews 8:12; 10:17). Those two little words—"no more"—cover a huge range of history and geography. God's Word tells us that our sins are washed clean (Isaiah 1:18), thrown into the depths of the sea (Micah 7:19), and put behind God's back (Isaiah 38:17).

Since this is God's perspective of our sins, how should we regard them? If we neglect the freedom and forgiveness that he offers us, then we ignore the power of the blood of Jesus given for us on the cross. Indeed, we could say that we almost abuse Christ's sacrifice. Scripture says, "If we confess our sins, he is faithful and just and will forgive us our sins and purify us from all unrighteousness" (1 John 1:9). That's the condition for God's choice of amnesia. The blood of Jesus has made us to be just as if we had never sinned. The price for our sins has been paid; and when God forgives, God forgets.

We have no right to try to remember that which God has forgotten. Think deeply about this. We often embrace our guilt and the memory of our sins, but that is not what God wants us to remember. For having been forgiven by our Lord, he wants us to forgive ourselves—and move on. Like Thomas, Peter, and Moses, we have encountered a God who uniquely provides us with a second chance. He gives us the opportunity to realize that we are forgiven and to start again. We are not just free to live a new life; we have a responsibility to appropriate this new life and to live in a new direction.

Live Beneath the Cross

Does that mean there is no further judgment on our lives? Having now crossed over from death to life, are we absolved from any responsibility for our conduct here on earth? Now that we are living with the privilege of God's magnificent forgiveness, is there no assessment of how we employ those gifts and graces that God has so freely entrusted to us?

Jesus told simple stories about rulers and businessmen who traveled away from home but assigned their servants the task of maximizing the capital resources left with them. Accountability was built into the arrangement. Each was expected to invest and increase what he received (Matthew 25:14–30; Luke 19:11–27). One failed to do so. He just hid what was entrusted to him, and consequently he was condemned for his laziness, fear, and lack of initiative.

Should we think that the Master would expect any less from his faithful servants today—once we have viewed the cross of Jesus? Once we have been introduced to the reality of the crucified life? Once we have understood the implications of exchanging our lives for his?

When we have come to this point, then each of us must face the big question: How are we to live? How do we fulfill the glorious purpose that God has for our lives?

A couple of years ago, Ruth and I closed a chapter of our lives. We proudly watched as our youngest child graduated from seminary—and we knew that the era of school expenses was over! This was a great moment for Suzy: graduating and then beginning a position as worship leader at a Baptist church in Wisconsin.

The chapel at the London School of Theology was too small to accommodate the graduation ceremony. A nearby church, Soul Survivor, was meeting in a large converted gymnasium and allowed the seminary to use its facility for the occasion.

The retired Archbishop of Canterbury, Dr. George Carey, presented the academic achievement awards. Before fulfilling this duty, he was invited to take two or three minutes to make some comments. Another speaker would subsequently deliver the formal address, which he did quite well. It is Dr. Carey's comments, however, that will remain etched in my memory.

He quietly stood at the podium placed in the front of this vast gymnasium. There were no stained glass windows and no altar, just a simple wooden cross suspended from the ceiling directly above where Dr. Carey stood. He made only three comments. First he expressed his gratitude for the honor of presenting the awards, then he congratulated those preparing to receive their degrees. Finally he paused for a moment before making his last remark. He pointed to the cross above him, gazed at the expectant faces of the graduates, and said, "You will come now and graduate beneath the cross. Live there; live there."

My guess is that neither Suzy nor those who graduated with her will ever forget those words. Live beneath the cross; never move away from where God has brought you.

Scripture warns that all people will stand before the judgment seat of Christ to explain their actions in this life (Matthew 12:36; Romans 14:10; 2 Corinthians 5:10). Christians may quickly respond that this warning no longer applies to them. After all, "Whoever believes in [Christ] is not condemned" (John 3:18). The prophet Micah asked, "Who is a God like you, who pardons sin and forgives the transgression of the remnant of his inheritance?" (Micah 7:18). The apostle Paul observed,

"Therefore, there is now no condemnation for those who are in Christ Jesus" (Romans 8:1).

Clearly we are acquitted in the judgment pertaining to salvation. But what about our lives and actions after we meet Jesus? Paul instructed the Corinthian church to judge themselves so that they would not be subsequently judged (1 Corinthians 11:27–33). He also warned the church in Rome to be ready to give an account of themselves to God (Romans 14:12). This echoed Jesus' solemn statement, "From everyone who has been given much, much will be demanded; and from the one who has been entrusted with much, much more will be asked" (Luke 12:48).

In this sense, we are not totally free from the implications of God's law. Yet neither are we weighed down by the demanding law revealed to Moses. Instead, we live up to the family expectations of a Father's heart. This is what he requires from those whose lives are surrendered to Jesus and who want to live beneath the cross.

This judgment concerns how we have lived within the family of God. As A. W. Tozer has pointedly observed, "One day our record will be examined for evidence of our faithfulness, self-discipline, generosity beyond the demands of the law, courage before our detractors, humility, separation from the world, cross carrying . . ."[1]

In this judgment, our careless words will be evaluated (Matthew 12:36), our secret sins exposed (Romans 2:16), and

---

1. A. W. Tozer, *The Radical Cross* (Camp Hill, PA: Wing Spread Publishers, 2006), 83.

the quality of our ministry for Christ assessed. Then we will discover if gold and silver or wood and straw were the final result of our labors (1 Corinthians 3:9–15). We know that we could never meet God's standards without Christ. We need to live each day beneath the cross.

Living in Light of Heaven

We can deduce, based on the biblical evidence, that there is one judgment for salvation and another judgment for how our hearts were conformed to Christ, including our service for him. The latter verdict does not qualify us for heaven, but it can determine what reception we will receive upon our arrival there. This may sound rather frightening. We always need to remember, however, that the record is not of what we have done for Christ, but of what we have allowed him to achieve *through us*.

If all our human efforts are totally inadequate to prepare us for heaven, then what would happen if we released the power of God in our lives here on earth? The focus on why we are still here shifts when we recognize that our potential to serve *began* when we surrendered to Jesus—it did not end there! Suddenly the significance and values others urge upon us diminish in importance as we begin to live in light of the place where we will give account for our lives: the judgment seat of Christ.

Some of us are reluctant to examine our lives with the honesty with which Jennifer has evaluated hers. If we do, however, then we can know—as she did—the awesome wonder of God's forgiveness and healing in those hidden but sacred places of our hearts and lives.

Jennifer did not feel it was enough to lay back in her illness and prepare to meet her Lord. The idea of hanging on for heaven was not in her understanding. She was ready to meet him, but first she wanted to serve him out of gratitude for all that he had done for her. She may have missed opportunities, but she has made powerful use of her remaining time; and one day she will stand before the living God, knowing the joy of the harvest of hearts she led into his family.

We cannot earn our way into heaven. What we can do is offer ourselves to God now, live in the way he intends, and then enter heaven with fewer regrets than would otherwise be the case. At that point God will amaze us by giving us the praise that he promises for faithful service (1 Corinthians 4:5). In the meantime, the greater our surrender, the more God's love and power will be at work in us. It's our motives that God examines and his praise that we can anticipate!

Standing Before the Throne

We do not need to stop with motives only. Pause for a moment and try to grasp that God reviews the desires of our hearts—and he responds to those desires. The passion in our hearts to love and serve Jesus will produce results, not just a mental checklist of good intentions.

Not wasting our lives really means being prepared to live for the benefit of others. It means springing into action to meet the needs of the poor, the hurting, the lonely, and the oppressed around the world—and especially on our own doorstep (Matthew 25:31–40). It also means that we recognize the urgency to share the love of Jesus through the way we live and by telling people the good news about Jesus (Matthew 28:18–20).

The call the Lord places on our lives is a challenge to love him and develop a deep, intimate relationship with him. That call expands to love our community in all its lostness and need, and to love and support God's people worldwide as they seek to reach their nations for Jesus. The motive is crucial, but then actions will result.

A word of caution is required here: we can burn out because of our acts of kindness and service, actually achieving very little. The real desire of our hearts should not lie in what we do for others, but in how we serve our Lord and King. We must be careful to refrain from work that he doesn't command. One task done under divine direction and in the power of the Holy Spirit is worth more than a thousand well-intentioned, worthy activities.

A crucified life is lived to please God. An exchanged life will allow him to work through us. Rather than using the best that we can offer, we are called to allow our God to lead, mobilize, direct, and empower so that all is done with, through, and for him.

There is a great story about a young piano student who was discovered by a London impresario. This talent scout was so enamored by the young man's abilities that he decided to offer him the opportunity of a lifetime. The music student found himself seated behind a grand piano, playing to an enthusiastic crowd that had packed a London concert hall to enjoy a free performance that evening. The generous impresario had paid for everything.

Filled with gratitude and an understanding of how far this amazing opportunity could lead, the young man played brilliantly. The music he produced that night was incredible. He truly gave his audience the performance of a lifetime. A British audience can be cautious, to put it charitably, in giving praise. But not that night! To the impresario's amazement, the spectators spontaneously rose to their feet and clapped and cheered.

As the young pianist left the platform, he was enthusiastically greeted by the impresario, who said, "Go on, play an encore!"

The young man shook his head.

"But they are all standing for you," urged the impresario.

"No, they are not," the young man responded. "That old man seated on the aisle three rows from the back of the balcony . . . See him? He's sitting."

"Only one—he cannot know his music!" was the impresario's verdict.

"Oh yes he does," came the reply. "That's my teacher. If he was standing and everyone else was sitting, then I would play an encore. But I can't if he's still sitting."

Dr. R. T. Kendall shared with me a marvelous epilogue to this story. Two thousand years ago, a man named Stephen died. As he was about to be stoned to death for his faith in Jesus, the face of this first martyr lit up as he saw Jesus waiting in heaven for him. Then, as Jesus had done, Stephen forgave his killers before he died. Scripture tells us that our Lord Jesus is seated at the right hand of the Father. But that is not how Stephen saw him. Jesus was standing (Acts 7:55)—standing for one who had lived for him and would now die for him.

Whether or not we are called to be martyrs, we too die in order to live. That's the paradox of the crucified life.

So do not waste your life. If you have already surrendered your life to Jesus, then heaven waits. The question remains: Will Jesus be standing or sitting when you arrive to meet him?

I long with all of my heart to be part of a church that gets Jesus standing—standing because we lived and died for him and did not waste our lives sitting back and comfortably anticipating heaven. Instead, we allowed him to live and love through us to *touch* and *change* his world.

Let the last word belong to the Lord Jesus himself: "Behold, I am coming soon! My reward is with me, and I will give to everyone according to what he has done" (Revelation 22:12).

Prayer ▶ Lord, you know that I am not in this just for the final rewards. I long to live for you and to know that you are living through me in a way that really makes a difference. Take me to the front lines of the work of your kingdom. Fill my heart with the joy and wonder of seeing the bold and wonderful things that you yearn to do—and let your still, small voice guide me to those who have no voice of their own. Soften my heart until I sense that when I minister to others, I minister to you. May I not waste the opportunity, in the time I have left on earth, to surrender all I have and am in return for all your grace, guidance, and empowerment. Thank you, Father. Amen.